Battles and Battlefields

David Scott Daniell describes fifteen of the
most important battles fought in Britain, from
Stamford Bridge in 1066 to Culloden in 1746.
Each vivid account is based on surviving
records and illustrated by strategic maps, so
that the visitor to the sites of the old battle-
fields can imagine for himself the exact position
of the opposing forces and the way in which the
fighting progressed.
David Scott Daniell also wrote novels for
children and adults, regimental histories and
radio and TV plays.

Battles
and
Battlefields

David Scott Daniell

Illustrations and Maps by William Stobbs

Beaver Books

First published in 1961 by
B. T. Batsford Limited
4 Fitzhardinge Street, Portman Square
London W1H 0AH

This paperback edition published in 1976 by
The Hamlyn Publishing Group Limited
London · New York · Sydney · Toronto
Astronaut House, Feltham, Middlesex, England

© Copyright Text David Scott Daniell 1961
© Copyright Illustrations B. T. Batsford Limited 1961
ISBN 0 600 31404 9

Printed in England by Cox & Wyman Limited
London, Reading and Fakenham
Set in Fournier

Introduction

Battles in Britain

A battle is an awe-inspiring and a terrible event, no matter whether it be fought with sword, lance, pike and cross-bow; musket, sabre and cannon; or machine-gun, high velocity shells and tanks and aircraft. In battle a large number of men fight each other to the death; many are killed, many wounded. War is ugly, battle is brutal.

Yet there is another side to it, which does not alter the main fact that war and battle are horrible. In battle men willingly risk death or mutilation for what they believe to be right. One would not say that every soldier who has fought in battle went voluntarily, or even understood what he was fighting for. Yet there are always some, often many, who fight and kill for what they believe to be a just cause. Ordinary men become inspired to unexpected heights of courage and become selfless. Many a man has fought willingly, and died without complaining, because he sincerely believed he was fighting for the freedom of others, of people he would never know, of generations unborn.

Battles are violent and tremendous events, they are the key points of history. The Norman conquest was made by the battle of Hastings, our much-prized form of government by free parliament was confirmed by the battle of Naseby. One could cite a score of examples. Battles are important, and because they are essentially human stories of life and death, of utmost endeavour, and because they often have far-reaching results, they make good reading.

A battle does not happen suddenly; it is the climax of events in which the difference of opinion has become so sharp that it is resolved by fighting. To understand why 10,000 men face each other on a battle-field it is necessary to understand the quarrel which brought them to that place.

The stories in this book, all about battles fought in Britain, begin with the cause of the quarrel, so that by the time the armies face each other we know why they are there, for what they are fighting and who are the commanders. Without that knowledge a battle is meaningless.

This book tells the stories of fifteen battles, beginning in 1066 and ending in 1746. There are many more, as the list on pages 185–7 shows. There were famous battles between Romans and Britons, and between the Saxons and the Vikings, notably King Alfred's victory at Ethandun in 878. But the information for these earlier battles is sketchy and in most cases experts cannot agree over the details. The year 1066 seems to be a good starting-point, especially as it is the one date we all know.

Most of the battles we have included are of Englishmen against Englishmen, or Scots or Irish, and the prize is the crown, though at Edgehill and Naseby it was to decide who should govern, king or parliament. The first two battles in the book are against foreign invaders; we won the first and lost the second. There is some consolation in the fact that although Duke William of Normandy conquered our island, he and his Normans became English.

William's invasion in 1066 was the last time anyone has succeeded, though there have been other attempts: Philip of Spain in 1588, Napoleon in 1805, and Hitler of Germany in 1940. The first two were foiled by the Royal Navy, defeating the Armada, and the combined French and Spanish fleets at Trafalgar. The last attempt was foiled by the gallantry of the fighters of the Royal Air Force. Fighting against tremendous odds, they saved us in the Battle of Britain. We have not included that great battle in this book because it was fought in the skies and not on the soil of Britain.

Battles are noisy, bewildering affairs, often confused and always confusing to the soldiers themselves. There is the mad din of battle, shouts and cries, the clash of steel, the explosion of muskets and cannon, or the deadly ripple of rifle or machine gun and the whistle of bullets. Remember the background of noise, the dust, the colour of uniforms, the shouting when you read the story of a battle. No words can properly describe a battle; the reader must do his share.

Contents

Contents

Chapter 1

Harold Saves His Kingdom

The Battle of Stamford Bridge

25th September 1066

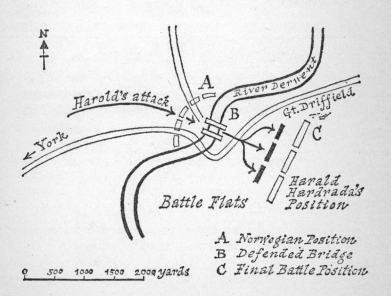

N

Harold's attack

York

A

River Derwent

B

Gt. Driffield

C

Battle Flats

Harald Hardrada's Position

A Norwegian Position
B Defended Bridge
C Final Battle Position

0   500   1000   1500   2000   yards

The death of King Edward the Confessor in January, 1066, brought England to a vital turning-point in her history. The year 1066 is the one date every Englishman knows; rightly so, because it is the year of the Norman conquest, which changed the character of the race. As the generations passed after the conquest, English blood, already a strong mixture of British, Roman, Saxon and Danish, was further enriched with the Norman strain. A race was bred which was destined, small though its island was, to become a great world power.

The events of that famous year sprang from the fact that Edward the Confessor left no son to succeed him. His heir was a boy, his nephew, Edgar the Atheling. In those turbulent days Might was Right, and a boy stood little chance of holding a throne amid the rival factions which would soon be up in arms. Apart from young Edgar, there were four possible successors to the throne of England. They were Harold Godwinson, Earl of Wessex; his elder brother Tostig, once Earl of Northumberland but banished; King Harald Hardrada of Norway; and William, Duke of Normandy. Each had a claim, and each was warrior enough to fight for it and, if victorious, to hold his crown by might.

King Edward named Harold Godwinson his heir on his death-bed. The choice was enthusiastically confirmed by the Witan, the great council of nobles, and Harold was quickly crowned king. He knew well that his rivals would not meekly accept his succession, and he immediately prepared to deal with the inevitable invasions. He had a double advantage; he was accepted by the English and he was already crowned king.

Invasions could be expected on the south coast by William of Normandy, on the north-east coast by Harald Hardrada of Norway, and across the border from Scotland, by Tostig, for Harold's banished brother had found an ally in the king of Scotland. Harold set his fleet patrolling between Dover and the Isle of Wight, to intercept an invasion fleet from France, and posted scouts on the coast. In the north, the Earls Morcar of Northumbria and his brother Edwin of Mercia stood ready at York with an army to repel Harald Hardrada or Tostig.

Harold stayed in London, ready to march north or south, with his regular force of Danish housecarls and the fyrd, men called up for the emergency. The housecarls were recognised as the finest infantry in Europe. They were the king's bodyguard, a proud and finely disciplined corps which provided the nucleus of his army.

Harold waited throughout the spring and summer of 1066 poised ready to spring into action when the alarm was given. The long and anxious wait ended in the third week in September, when messengers from the north brought Harold the news that his northern enemies had combined. Hardrada had sailed with a large fleet from Norway to the mouth of the River Tyne, where, by arrangement, he was joined by Tostig's fleet and army. Together they sailed down the coast, up the Humber estuary, and into the River Ouse, to disembark at Riccall, ten miles south of York. Harald Hardrada had left his young son Olaf with a guard over the ships and had set out for York.

Harold acted at once. He sent messengers ahead to rally the fyrd and set off up the Roman road for York. His troops were infantry, but for speed they rode on ponies. One remark of Harold's when he heard that Hardrada had landed has come down to us across the thousand years. The messenger told him that Hardrada had come to conquer all of England. Harold replied: 'I will give him just six feet of English soil; or, since they say he is a tall man, I will give him seven feet!'

Harold marched swiftly north, the army growing at every town they passed through. They reached Tadcaster on the 24th September, four days after leaving London, and here Harold received bad news. Earls Morcar and Edwin had faced the invaders at Fulford, two and a half miles south of York, and had been utterly defeated. The earls were in York with the remnants of their army, the city was ready to surrender and acknowledge Harald Hardrada as king, and the invading army was encamped ten miles east of York. Harold quickened his pace.

The English army entered York at dawn on the 25th September, having covered a hundred and ninety-two miles in five days. Many commanders would have paused at York to rest and prepare for battle, but not so Harold of England. His enemy was encamped only two hours' march away, and there was a fine opportunity of taking the Norsemen by surprise. So, after only an hour's rest, Harold led his army eastwards from York.

Harald Hardrada's army was encamped on either side of the River Derwent, where it was crossed by Stamford Bridge. They were so unprepared for the arrival of Harold that they had left their body-armour with their fleet, twelve miles away at Riccall. Suddenly somebody noticed a cloud of dust two miles away – the English army. Hardrada called a hasty council of war. Tostig recommended immediate retreat to Riccall, but with the enemy so close that would have been hazardous. The plan made was for one-third of the army to remain on the west bank of the river to delay Harold from crossing, while the rest formed up in flat meadowland beyond the river, known now as Battle Flats. The bustle and scramble of the Norsemen so suddenly surprised can well be imagined.

Harold sent messengers ahead offering peace to his brother Tostig if he would bring his men away from the Norse army. Tostig refused, probably because, surrounded as he was by the Norsemen, he could do nothing else.

Harold attacked at once and battle was joined on the west bank

The heroic Norseman holding Stamford Bridge

of the Derwent. The English made rapid progress, driving the enemy back across Stamford Bridge or into the river itself. The Derwent was deep and its bottom muddy, and many Norsemen were drowned as they tried to cross. Hardrada's main army was meanwhile forming up in Battle Flats, where the contest would be decided, and they were given an unexpected respite by the heroism of one Norseman.

This unnamed hero acted as Horatio did in ancient Rome against the hosts of Tarquin. He stood alone on the English side of Stamford Bridge and, swinging his heavy sword, denied the crossing until the ground before him was ringed with dead English. He seemed to bear a charmed life as he fought off his assailants. The bridge was eventually cleared by a clever ruse. An English soldier found a wash-tub, part of the Norsemen's camp equipment. He put it in the river, got into it, and handed himself down the bank to the bridge. Then, standing in his wash-tub boat, he was behind the Norseman, who was too occupied fighting valiantly against all comers to see his danger from the rear. Thus was the hero struck down and the bridge was at last open for the English to surge across to the eastern bank, to face Harald Hardrada's main force.

The Norsemen were formed up in a solid phalanx awaiting the inevitable onslaught, Harald Hardrada in the centre beneath his banner, the Land Ravager. Harold formed his battle line on the east bank of the Derwent and as soon as they were ready led them straight at the mass of Norsemen in a furious charge. The Norsemen received the charge unshaken, and there was violent infighting as the clash of battle-axe and sword, war cries and oaths, rose in the din of battle. Try as they might, the English could not break the Norsemen's line, and soon they fell back to get their breath.

Harold then adopted the same ruse which was to lead to his downfall three weeks later. Holding back his main force, he launched an attack with a small force on the Norsemen's flank, telling his men that after a brief spell of fighting they should break and fly as if in panic. The plan worked as Harold had hoped.

When the English ran away, crying aloud in mock dismay, the Norsemen could not resist the temptation and they went after them in pursuit, breaking Harald's solid line. Harold ordered his English archers to shoot high at the main body of the enemy. The retreating English turned suddenly and fought their pursuers and, at the same moment, while the main body of Norsemen defended themselves as best they could from the flights of arrows that were falling among them, Harold led his housecarls in another charge. This time the charge went home, and the Norsemen broke. There was more furious fighting with battle-axe and sword, but the Norsemen, their close lines broken, were borne back. Then a falling arrow pierced Harald Hardrada's throat, and he fell dead.

The battle was not over yet, however. Again the English fell back and paused for breath. Tostig assumed command and tried desperately to rally the Norsemen. Before they could form up again, however, King Harold led a third charge, and this time it won the victory. Tostig was slain, and the Norsemen fled towards their ships at Riccall, nine miles away. Many were cut down as they ran until Harold called back his men, content with his victory. The proud banner, the Land Ravager, was his. Both Hardrada and Tostig were dead. The survivors of the invading army were scattered.

Harold dealt mercifully with the vanquished foe. Young Olaf was spared and he and the remnants of the army were allowed to sail back to Norway. But before they went Harold extracted a promise from Olaf: that never again would Norsemen invade England. Thus Harold, at the battle of Stamford Bridge, ended once and for all the threat from the Norsemen, a threat which had existed for six centuries. Two of the challengers to Harold's crown had been dealt with, and both were buried in the seven feet of English soil that Harold had promised Hardrada.

Chapter 2

William Conquers England

The Battle of Hastings

14th October 1066

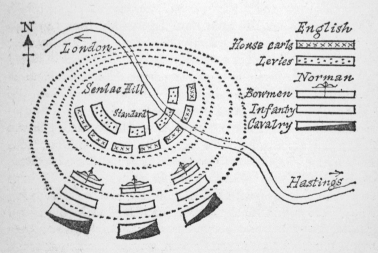

At the battle of Stamford Bridge King Harold quelled the invasion in the north and slew two of his rivals for the crown of England. There remained one more – Duke William of Normandy. William struck swiftly, and within a week of Harold's victory at Stamford Bridge, when the king was celebrating his victory at a great banquet in York, came the news that the Norman army had landed on the south coast.

Harold was a man of swift action. Messengers were sent in all directions to the south calling on Englishmen to rally to his standard in London. Harold left York at the head of his army, sadly thinned by casualties at Stamford Bridge, and marched rapidly down the Roman road to give battle to William of Normandy.

Duke William had protested loudly when Harold had succeeded King Edward the Confessor as king of England, claiming that the succession was his. His claim was three-fold: royal blood, a promise of the succession from King Edward, and an oath sworn by Harold two years before. His claim to royal blood was but slight, but so was Harold's. William's claim that King Edward had promised him the succession may have been true, but there seems to have been no witness. His third claim, that Harold had admitted William's right on oath, was real enough, although Harold claimed that the oath had been forced from him.

Harold, then Earl of Wessex, was shipwrecked off the coast of

France in 1064 and held to ransom by the Count of Ponthieu. He was rescued by Duke William, for he and Harold were friends. Harold spent several months with William as his guest. They hunted together and Harold went with William on a short campaign. One day Duke William asked Harold to swear a solemn oath that when Edward the Confessor died William should succeed as king of England and that Harold would support him and continue as Earl of Wessex. Harold swore the oath on an altar; it is difficult to see how he could have refused while he was in William's hands; it was his only chance of being allowed to go home to England. To make doubly sure, William had deposited sacred relics of a saint underneath the altar, unknown to Harold. Thus the oath was completely binding, though the trick made it easier for Harold subsequently to forswear it.

In view of this oath, Duke William was very angry when he heard early in 1066 that Harold had been proclaimed and crowned king of England. He advertised the justice of his claim throughout western Europe and announced his intention to take an army and win the kingdom. He organised his campaign most thoroughly. Ships were built in every port along the western coast of France. William invited noblemen and knights to join his expedition, promising all who helped him a share in the spoils, a piece of England, the size according to the number of men or amount of money provided. No prince outside Normandy formally backed William's claim to England, but very many accepted his offer and joined the venture.

William's army mustered at St Valèry in August. He had cast his net wide and there were knights from nearly every country in western Europe, even from as far away as Italy. It was the flower of the chivalry of western Europe, all eager for the spoils to be gained by helping William to conquer England. The total was about twelve thousand, four thousand of them knights and men-at-arms with their trained war horses. The eight thousand infantry included several thousand excellent archers. The ships were ready, the men, horses and arms were ready, but for six weeks contrary winds kept the powerful army in France.

At last the wind changed, the great fleet sailed, and on the 28th September it reached Pevensey Bay, five miles east of modern Eastbourne and fifteen west of Hastings. The landing was un-opposed, for Harold's fleet, which had been patrolling between the Isle of Wight and Dover throughout the spring and early summer, had returned to the Thames to refit. As we have seen, King Harold and his army were nearly three hundred miles away recovering from their victory at Stamford Bridge three days before.

When William stepped ashore from his boat he tripped and fell flat on his face, to the alarm of his companions who saw it as an ill omen. Men set great store by omens in those days, but William had the knack of always being able to turn them in his favour. He got up, brushed off the sand, and said cheerfully, 'You see, my friends, I have already taken possession of England.' He showed the same quick wit two weeks later, on the morning of the battle of Hastings. His page put his armour on back to front, probably because he was over-excited at the prospect of battle. Those present were horrified, seeing it as an omen of defeat, but William rose to the occasion. As the armour was changed he said, 'You see what this means. It means that today I shall change my dukedom for a kingdom.'

William did not advance on London at once, as might have been expected. Instead, he built defences round Pevensey Bay to protect his fleet, made camp, and for two weeks sent out maraud-ing columns into Kent and Sussex. These columns behaved with great cruelty, destroying villages and butchering all the English they caught. The news of the Normans' barbarism did them grave disservice, for it made the angry English hurry to join Harold. It would have been wiser for William, coming to 'liberate' England from a man he described as a usurper, to have behaved benevolently; but there was no sign of any benevolence.

Harold reached London seven days after he left York. He stayed in the capital for five days to rest. This was necessary, for his men had marched from London to York, fought a very hard battle, and had marched back again. While they rested, new troops hurried into London and took their places in the army. This was the fyrd, men bound to become soldiers when the king called on them. Their leaders were the theigns, the 'squires' or gentry who held land under the king on condition that they provided a special number of armed men when called upon. The theigns and their men were well armed, the rest of the fyrd indifferently so.

Messengers from William offered terms for a settlement, but Harold would not consider any terms. His natural anger at William's invasion was increased to rage by reports he received of wholesale murder of unarmed English in Kent and Sussex, so much so that he marched south from London on the 13th October while large numbers of armed men were still marching from the north and west to join him.

Harold took the direct route to Pevensey Bay and halted eight miles short on a bare hill then marked only by an old apple tree, now famous as Senlac Hill. Here Harold set up his two standards – the Dragon of Wessex, and his own personal standard, the Fighting Man. Senlac Hill stood astride William's road to London. It is a bold feature one hundred and ten yards long and about one hundred and fifty yards in depth. To the south it slopes down gradually, whilst at the north, the descent is steep except for a narrow isthmus which carries the London road. The army camped there that night, expecting battle on the morrow.

During the night Harold's scouts brought the news that the Norman army was preparing to march from Pevensey, and it was clear that the battle to decide who should be king of England, Harold or William, was to be fought on the 14th October. The date seemed of good omen, for it was Harold's birthday, and before dawn, on the certain news the Normans were marching towards him, he set his army in battle array.

The famous housecarls, perhaps two thousand strong, formed the front line, about one-third to the east of the standards and two-thirds to the west of them. These splendid fighters, armed with chain mail to the knees and wearing pointed helmets to deflect the blow of weapons, carried long kite-shaped shields. Standing as close together as they could, leaving room to wield their heavy two-handed battle-axes, the shields presented a long and formidable shield-wall. It was this shield-wall, and the valour of the men behind it, which barred William's road to London, and to the conquest of England.

The fyrd was posted on the flanks of the line, with the theigns and their well-armed men in front and the rest of the fyrd, civilians turned soldier for the occasion, massed in ranks ten or twelve deep to the rear. The untrained part of the fyrd had armed themselves as best they could, with swords, javelins, throwing axes, bows, iron-studded clubs and even scythes, reaping hooks and hay forks. The English line followed the shape of the hill, turning back on the flanks to form a wide curve. A number of housecarls were grouped about King Harold and the standards as his personal royal bodyguard.

The Norman army marched up the road to London for half a dozen miles until they came in sight of Senlac Hill, where the long shield-wall barred their way, and the massed spears of the English gave the appearance of a thick wood. William halted and deployed his army in line just west of the London road and some six hundred yards from Senlac Hill. The Normans were formed into three divisions, each in the same formation; first the archers, behind them the infantry, and in the rear the mounted and armoured knights and men-at-arms. As they took up their positions, the Normans put on their chain mail. The English stood fast on their hill, watching and waiting.

King Harold's plan was to stand defiantly athwart the road to London, daring the invader to try to get through. He was confident that his housecarls, backed by the massed soldiers of the fyrd, would be able to beat off the Normans as a cliff repels the assaults of the sea. He knew that if his line stood fast the armoured enemy attacking up the hill must eventually tire. Then, and only then, would be the time to advance down the hill and destroy them.

Harold's orders were clear and simple: the line must remain unbroken, however furious the attack, however tempting it would be to pursue when the Normans were thrown back; all depended on the resolution of the English line, which must never be broken, either by onslaught or by pursuit.

The battle of Hastings began about half past nine on the morning of the 14th October, 1066. As modern battles commence with an artillery bombardment to 'soften' the enemy, so William opened with the bowmen. The Norman archers advanced to within one hundred yards of the English and released a whistling cloud of arrows. The English raised their long shields and received the bombardment without flinching. There were casualties, but the gaps were closed and the line remained unbroken.

William then ordered his foot soldiers forward. They advanced up the hill into a furious fusillade of arrows, javelins, and heavy throwing-clubs and light axes. A number fell, but the advance was sustained, and, yelling their war cries, the Norman infantry threw itself against the English line. It was fierce hand-to-hand fighting. The Normans swung their long double-edged swords, the English their battle-axes. Helmets were split, or sword or axe glanced off the helmet and was buried in the enemy's shoulder.

The English line stood firm and gradually the impetus of the Norman attack began to ebb. On their left the Normans broke off the fight, and promptly received a heavy shower of javelins and clubs. They turned and ran down the hill. Soon the whole Norman line was in retreat, sent off with missiles and the derisive shouts of the English. Harold's housecarls rested on their battle-axes, but the sight of the running enemy was too much for the undisciplined soldiers of the fyrd on the English right. In spite of Harold's orders they broke ranks and, yelling in triumph, pursued the foe.

The Normans were in grave danger. As the infantry ran down the hill, pursued by their triumphant enemy on the English right, panic spread, made worse by the shouted rumour that Duke William was killed. Only prompt action by William stopped the panic; throwing off his helmet, he rode among his demoralised men, urging them to stand and form up again. The sight of their leader and his vigorous commands steadied them. They checked their retreat and turned, to be sorted into proper formation again.

At the same time William called forward a body of his cavalry and pointed out the English who, having pursued the Normans down the hill, were engaged in hand-to-hand combat with them. The cavalry wheeled and bore down upon the fighting men. The Norman infantry fell back, and the English were butchered. Only a handful managed to regain the line at the top of the hill.

It was then about noon, and there was a pause for an hour or more, necessary to men fighting in heavy chain mail. On Senlac Hill, Harold sent men to fetch water and food. Dead and wounded were taken to the rear, and the Norman weapons were carefully collected from the ground. The arrows were shared out among the bowmen; swords, spears and battle-axes to men who needed them.

The Normans rested too, and drank and ate what rations they had with them. The line was re-formed and Duke William considered the problem of how to break that resolute shield-wall on the hill. He had used his archers and his foot soldiers, and both had failed. He had still his mounted men, highly trained knights, and the men-at-arms, all protected with chain mail, all experienced in battle on the Continent and mounted on heavy well-trained war horses. He had intended to keep them back for the pursuit when the English line was broken. But the line was still intact. Surely, he thought, these would smash the English line.

The interval was ended with the sound of the Norman horns and the foot soldiers opened their ranks to let the horsemen ride through. The English, refreshed and reorganised, braced themselves for the attack. Led by Duke William himself, the long line of some four thousand horsemen trotted towards the hill, the heavy two-handed swords shining in the afternoon sun.

Harold's hill-top position, however, deprived the enemy of the main effect of a cavalry attack, the terrifying and well-nigh irresistible charge of a mass of galloping horses. The war horse of those days was like the heaviest cart horse of these days, and instead of being able to thunder down on the English they had to pick their way laboriously up the hill, into a hail of arrows, javelins, throwing-axes and heavy clubs.

Normans charging the English line on Senlac Hill, 1066

There is a legend, which may well be true, that as the Norman cavalry approached the English line a minstrel knight, Ivo Taillefer, galloped out in front, throwing his lance and sword high into the air and catching them with juggler's skill, and then charged straight at the English line. Bursting through, he was immediately hewn to pieces.

Behind this extraordinary, high-spirited minstrel knight, the mass of Norman cavalry rode towards the English line, where the housecarls waited with their axes raised. With their famous cry of 'Out! Out!' the battle-axes crashed down, felling horses and riders, as the long Norman swords swung down upon the English axe-men. The clash of steel on steel, the yells of the men, and the excited whinnying of the horses made an inferno of noise, the din of battle at its wildest. The slaughter on both sides was terrible, and among those who fell in this furious stage of the conflict were Harold's younger brothers, Gurth and Leofwyne.

Three times the Norman cavalry drew back to charge again. Twice Duke William's horse was killed under him, and he was to lose a third before the battle was over. But all was to no avail. The English line stayed firm across the road to London, though many men had to stand astride the dead. The two standards still flew, where King Harold, sword in hand, fought with his men.

Exhausted by the strenuous fighting, the Norman cavalry rode back down the hill, leaving a quarter of their number dead or dying on the hill-top. For the second time the sight of the defeated enemy going away was too much for some of the English and, this time the left of the line, the inexperienced soldiers of the fyrd dashed after them. The result was the same as before: a body of Norman horse wheeled and rode them down, and they were lost to Harold.

There was another pause. It was now late afternoon. The English line closed up; it was much shorter, from the heavy casualties and because of the troops from the flanks lost through disobedience of the king's orders. Dead and wounded were taken back, weapons were collected, and the battle-weary men, many of them wounded, stood staring at the enemy below them. They knew that it could not last much longer, for there is a limit to human endurance. All on Senlac Hill were resolved that it would not be they who gave in.

Duke William had failed to break the line with his bowmen, with his foot, and with his heavy armoured horsemen. He decided to use all three arms together in one last desperate attempt. He re-formed and ordered his bowmen to shoot their arrows high, to fall down on the English line. Under the protection of this barrage, the foot-soldiers and the men-at-arms could advance through the archers and attack. The knights and men-at-arms dismounted, to attack on foot, for the horses were exhausted. The English watched and waited, silently, making no move when the mass of men below them started to march yet again towards the hill.

The last phase of the battle of Hastings, fought as the dusk of the October evening closed down, was even more desperate than before. The deathly rain of Norman arrows which preceded the attack was taken, as before, on the uplifted shields, but many found their mark. As soon as the Norman archers ceased to shoot, the mass of mixed knights, men-at-arms and spearmen surged up the hill and fell upon the line. Again axe and sword rang on steel.

The English line remained as firm as it had done throughout the long day, but now it was shorter; before the flanks had curved round the hill-top, now there was a wide gap at each end. This enabled the Normans to attack the flanks as well as the front. Every man in those two battle-weary hosts was giving his utmost. Gradually the two wings of the English line were turned back against the flank attacks. Foremost among the attackers, trying to fight his way through to the two standards, was Duke William.

Then occurred an evil turn of fortune. The Norman archers who had arrows left were still shooting, their range lengthened so that their arrows fell among the English at the rear of the line. One arrow, falling short, struck King Harold in the right eye. He pulled it out angrily and tried to fight on. But the wound was mortal, and soon he could only remain on his feet by leaning on his sword hilt, his head bowed. The grievous news spread among the English, and some of the fyrd began to waver, for if King Harold was dead what was there left to fight for? Not so with Harold's housecarls. Fighting to the front and to each flank, their line gradually grew shorter as they were remorselessly beaten back. They were forced into a ring around the two standards and their stricken king. No one asked for quarter, no one ceased to fight while life was in him.

In the deepening dusk the end came. With a sudden surge a body of Norman men-at-arms broke through that gallant ring. A sword flashed and bit deep into King Harold's thigh, and he fell to the ground and died. So ended the proud line of Saxon kings, fighting to the last on Senlac Hill.

None of the housecarls left their king. The fyrd, who were only armed civilians, slipped away quickly to the thick woods behind the hill. Many of the Normans who pursued them, unaware of the precipitous slope behind the hill and not seeing it in the dusk, fell and were killed by English who paused in their flight to do so. Inside the woods, individual English waited, sword in hand, to pounce upon the pursuing Normans. But soon the fugitives found safety, and the long day's battle was over. Duke William had won his kingdom.

The next day the dead were buried in deep pits, the spoils of battle distributed among the victors, and William took stock of the situation. He did not march at once to London, for some other champion might arise, and he was in no condition to fight another battle against so obstinate a foe. He needed to make good his victory.

He set out on a long round-about march, through Kent, Sussex, Surrey, Hampshire and Berkshire, where he crossed the Thames at Wallingford. He marched on through Buckinghamshire and Hertfordshire to Berkhampstead. Here he rested and received the Archbishop of York, a number of bishops and English noblemen, and his claim to the crown of England was accepted. That done, he marched in triumph to London and was crowned King William of England at Westminster on Christmas Day.

William had an abbey built on Senlac Hill, with the altar on the spot where Harold's standards flew and where he fell, and the ruins of Battle Abbey are there still. The battle of Hastings was fought a thousand years ago, yet we know more about that battle than many fought five hundred years later, for we have a most wonderful pictorial record in the Bayeux tapestry. This long length of embroidered linen tells the whole story in pictures. It was made twenty years after the battle, according to legend by William's wife, Queen Mathilda, but more probably by an unknown hand.

The tapestry begins with a picture of Edward the Confessor on his throne talking to Harold, and continues with Harold's voyage to France, his visit to William of Normandy, the swearing of the oath, Harold's coronation, and the appearance of a comet which both Harold and William took as a good omen. This was Halley's comet, which has been seen on other occasions, notably in 1861.

The Bayeux tapestry tells the whole story of the invasion; William's preparations, the voyage and many pictures of the battle, down to the death of Harold. The tapestry, wonderfully preserved, is an enchanting record of those far-off days, and of the most important battle ever fought on English soil.

Chapter 3

Prince Edward Rescues His Father

The Battle of Evesham

4th August 1265

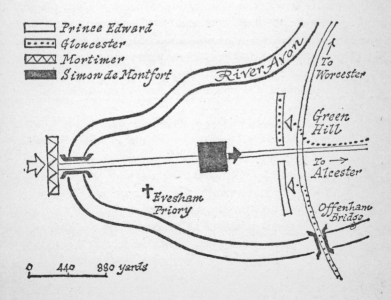

Prince Edward
Gloucester
Mortimer
Simon de Montfort

River Avon

To Worcester

Green Hill

To Alcester

✝ Evesham Priory

Offenham Bridge

0   440   880 yards

This is the story of the rescue of a king by his son. The king was Henry III, the son was Prince Edward, afterwards King Edward I, and the battle was fought at Evesham in Worcestershire in 1265, two centuries, all but one year, after the battle of Hastings. In those two centuries the Normans had become merged in the English race.

The Normans had established the feudal system, by which everyone in the country took his place in a rigorously maintained order. It was like a pyramid, with the king at the top. Immediately below him were the great nobles, owning their broad lands in return for the obligation of military service to the king. Next came the knights, owners of part of each baron's land, but holding their manors with duty for military service to the baron. So the layers of the pyramid broadened out to the base, the common people.

It was a well-ordered society in which everyone knew his place and his obligations. The higher the stratum in which you were born, the more comfortable it was. It put the king firmly at the top of the realm, with his authority reaching down to every subject through his barons, knights and yeomen.

One might wonder how in such an organised society a situation could arise in which it would be necessary for the king to be rescued. The reason is that even within the feudal system forces deeply characteristic of the English people were at work, springing from a natural instinct for justice and liberty. The king at the top of the great national pyramid was undoubtedly master of his realm, but even in the thirteenth century this authority did not go unquestioned.

The battle of Evesham, and its prelude at the battle of Lewes fifteen months before, sprang from the Englishman's deep-seated desire to have a say in the government of the country. It was not possible in feudal England for the ordinary man to influence affairs. Action came from the barons, the great land-owning nobles at the top of the pyramid. It was through them that the voice of the people was heard, and through them that a long quarrel was brought to violent action in battle.

Henry III, the king who was rescued from the power of the barons by his son, was the son of King John and grandson of Richard Lionheart. Henry succeeded his father as king in 1216, at the age of nine. He reigned for fifty-six years, the second longest reign in our history. King John had been forced to sign Magna Carta in 1215 but immediately denied it and took vengeance on the barons with foreign troops.

King John died. The barons brought out Magna Carta again when the young king was eighteen and old enough to act for himself and made him sign and confirm it. Thus the great principles of the rights of the individual to a fair trial, the main clause in Magna Carta, were established in England for all time, though they were not always observed. By signing Magna Carta, Henry III had given away part of the rights of a king, rights which had been enjoyed by his predecessors for two centuries. It was natural for him to try to win back those rights, and that was the prime cause of the conflict between himself and the barons throughout his long reign.

Henry was a mild, pleasant and pious man. He did not have the arrogant and unprincipled strength of his father, King John, nor the courage and military ability of the eldest son who later, as Edward I, conquered Wales and brought Scotland to the edge of subjection by sheer military genius. The mild King Henry strove to keep the barons in their place by diplomacy and intrigue.

The struggle for power between the king and the barons reached its climax in 1258. In that year a parliament, unjustly known as the 'Mad Parliament', met at Oxford and drew up what are known as the 'Provisions of Oxford'. These contained a suggestion which proved to be of the greatest importance in the history of England: that four knights should be chosen by each county to enquire into the wrongs committed by the king's councillors.

The Provisions of Oxford also asked that Parliament should meet three times in the year. The Parliament of those days consisted of the bishops, noblemen, and some knights. None of them was elected, and the Parliament in no way represented the people of England. The Provisions of Oxford produced a startling new idea, that some of the members of Parliament should be elected and so, as never before, represent the people, and be privileged to criticise the government of the king.

The king was not impressed by the Provisions of Oxford; Magna Carta was bad enough, this suggestion of a Parliament containing members coming up, as it were, from below and permitted to criticise the king's actions, seemed to him to spell disaster. He managed to put off any action for two years, and then he refused openly to take any notice of the Provisions of Oxford; he was king and he would rule the country as he wished. But the matter did not end there, for the barons were led by a remarkable man who holds a high place in the first rank of Englishmen, though he was, in fact, a Frenchman. This was Simon de Montfort, Earl of Leicester.

Simon de Montfort was born in Normandy, and when he grew up he agreed with his elder brother to exchange his share in the family estates for the earldom of Leicester in England, which had come to the family through Simon's English grandmother. Simon de Montfort came to England when he was twenty-four, and his claim to the earldom of Leicester was recognised by Henry III. His position was strengthened when he married the king's sister.

De Montfort was a lively and active young man who soon made his mark in his new country. He went on a crusade to the

Holy Land in 1240 and acted for the king on many important missions, including governing Gascony and later travelling to Scotland, France and Italy as ambassador. His knowledge of affairs, military ability and general importance made him the leader of the barons in their disputes with the king, and he helped to draw up the Provisions of Oxford. When the king refused to take any notice of the Provisions, Simon de Montfort took the lead in the next drastic step. The barons called their men to arms to force the king to carry out the Provisions of Oxford.

The king made his headquarters in the Midlands, while the barons held London and the south, as in the Civil War between Charles I and Parliament four centuries later. Henry III was no soldier, but in his brother Richard and his son Edward he had two very able lieutenants. The king's brother was an unusual man. He had fought with Simon de Montfort on the crusade of 1240 and had made a great name for himself. He was closely involved in European affairs, was offered and refused the German crown, and had been elected King of the Romans. He was an able, busy and warlike man, who entered into the conflict with the barons with zest. Prince Edward, although only twenty-four, had a natural grasp of military affairs.

Simon de Montfort had many of the qualities of that other champion of Parliament, Oliver Cromwell, who was to fight against his king four hundred years later. In addition to all the qualities of generalship, de Montfort, like Cromwell, had the gift of inspiring his men with that confidence which springs from deep belief in the rightness of their cause. He was also able to instil in his troops a discipline rare in medieval armies. The principal leaders under de Montfort were Gilbert de Clare, Earl of Gloucester, and Roger Mortimore, Baron of Wigmore.

The king took the initiative in the campaign and marched south from the Midlands. The armies met at Lewes on the 14th May, 1246, inland between Eastbourne and Hastings. The royal army was stronger in numbers than their enemy, but this was offset by the fact that de Montfort took the enemy by surprise and attacked before the royal army could be properly marshalled. In this de Montfort broke with the tradition of those days by which armies formed up and, as it were, sized each other up for a spell before engaging.

De Montfort introduced another unusual feature into the battle by marshalling his army into four divisions instead of the traditional three, keeping the fourth as a reserve. In both armies the divisions consisted of a mass of foot soldiers in six ranks behind squadrons of heavily armoured knights and men-at-arms. As the armies clashed together after the preliminary bombardment by each side of flights of arrows, Prince Edward broke the enemy line opposite him with a splendid cavalry charge, and, exulting in his victory, pursued the flying enemy. He pursued them so far that he went right out of the battle, thus depriving the king of cavalry which he sorely needed on the battlefield. Prince Rupert was to commit the same error at the battle of Edgehill four hundred years later.

Meanwhile, de Montfort's lightly armed Londoners were fighting violently against the fully equipped knights and infantry of the royal army. They had a double advantage: the royal army had not been fully prepared and de Montfort's men were raised far above themselves by the high morale with which they were inspired. Soon all three divisions of the king's army began to give ground, and de Montfort drove home the advantage by sending in his reserve division, fresh men eager to clinch the matter. First the royalist centre broke, and then the left flank. The king's horse was killed under him, and he was dragged away by his lifeguard and hurried to the nearby priory. Finally, the division on the right gave as well. Many of the royalist army were drowned in the marshland over which they tried to escape.

Simon de Montfort was completely victorious. The king was captured, and his brother, the King of the Romans, was found hiding in a windmill. Prince Edward was captured and taken to join his father at the priory. Simon de Montfort treated his royal prisoners with every respect. When they returned to London the king lived in his palace with his court, outwardly exactly as before. All deference due to a king was paid to him. The only difference was that the palace guards were de Montfort's men and the king acted, spoke, and signed as de Montfort told him to. Prince Edward also lived the same life as before the battle of Lewes, with the important exception that he could only go where de Montfort permitted, and then always attended by a deferential and discreet, but ever-vigilant-guard.

For ten months Simon de Montfort ruled England, though all was done in the name of the king. Whatever de Montfort wished, the king had to command. The prime cause of the battle of Lewes was the calling of a Parliament authorised – and this was the great novelty – to criticise the government of the king. Having won the battle, and with it the power to do as he wished, de Montfort had writs issued in the king's name summoning the new Parliament.

It was an historic occasion when this Parliament met in Westminster in 1265, for it contained citizens, 'Members of Parliament', two from each city and borough in the country. It was an immense step forward. Until then, and elsewhere in Europe, for several hundred years, kings ruled their lands as dictators, yet six hundred years ago England produced a Parliament containing elected representatives of the people, pointing the way to democratic government. For this great work the name of Simon de Montfort is ever honoured.

All was not as straightforward for de Montfort as it seemed, however, for not all the barons were prepared to recognise his authority, acting like a modern prime minister through the crown. Medieval barons were proud and quarrelsome. Each was a great magnate, ruling his own domains within the feudal system, and the overlord of all the knights and yeomen who owned land under him. Their power bred arrogance, and they did not easily recognise any authority but the king's.

There was unrest among a number of barons in the Welsh Marches, the wide stretch of land along the Welsh border. These 'Marcher Lords' found a leader in Roger Mortimer, Baron Wigmore. Mortimer had fought at Lewes for de Montfort, but after the battle he quarrelled with de Montfort and stormed off angrily to his castle at Wigmore. This is in Herefordshire, near

Ludlow and Leominster, and was a convenient gathering point for the dissatisfied 'Marcher Lords'.

The situation became worse for de Montfort when he quarrelled with Gilbert de Clare, Earl of Gloucester, who had commanded the centre division of de Montfort's army at Lewes and had been mainly responsible for the victory. Gloucester was the most powerful of all the barons, and his defection, due, it is said, to the arrogance of his sons, brought matters to a head. Gloucester left the court and went to his castle at Ludlow, only six miles from Mortimer at Wigmore. It must be remembered that at this time a baron could call on a considerable number of armed men through the knights on his land, each of whom was bound by law, when called upon, to bring all his armed men.

Simon de Montfort could not ignore this gathering storm in the west. He decided to take an army to deal with it. The only other serious problem was Pevensey Castle, which was held by a number of royalists who had taken refuge there after the battle of Lewes. De Montfort sent one of his sons, another Simon de Montfort, to besiege the castle while he dealt with the more serious trouble in the Welsh Marches.

In May, 1265, he marched at the head of his army, a force of five thousand or more, consisting of his own men and those of the barons who were still loyal to him. King Henry III and Prince Edward were taken with the army so that de Montfort would be seen to be acting for the king. He was also able to ensure the safety of the royal captives. De Montfort made his headquarters at Hereford, a convenient position from which to overawe the rebel barons or, if that failed, to march out to deal with them by force of arms.

On the 28th May Prince Edward was allowed to go hunting, with, of course, a large number of 'attendants', all de Montfort's men. From what followed it seems that the hunting trip was a carefully laid plan arranged by secret messages passed between the prince and Roger Mortimer. During the hunt, the prince suddenly set spurs to his horse and galloped ahead, pursued by his guards. He out-distanced them, met a confederate waiting with a fresh and very fast horse, leapt to the ground, jumped into the saddle of the new horse, and galloped away.

He rode hard, to the safety of Wigmore Castle, twenty miles away. With Mortimer, Prince Edward went to Ludlow, where the Earl of Gloucester was waiting. Gloucester and Mortimer did homage to the prince and raised their banners summoning all loyal men to join them to rescue the king from the hands of Simon de Montfort. The counties of Shropshire and Cheshire responded to the call, and the prince soon found himself at the head of a substantial and enthusiastic army.

De Montfort's first act was to make the king sign a decree outlawing Prince Edward, Gloucester and Mortimer. He had to decide what to do next: to attack the prince at once, to continue with his original plan of hunting down the rebel barons in the Marches and in Wales, or to fall back to occupy a central position at Worcester, closing the road from the west to London. He decided to continue with his original plan. Knowing subsequent events as we do, we can see that the decision was wrong, for it gave Prince Edward time to increase and organise his army and, more important, it gave him the initiative.

Prince Edward was only twenty-six years old, but was a born soldier. His campaign of the next three months was one of brilliant strategy. De Montfort was on the far side of the River Severn. The prince seized Bridgnorth and Worcester and destroyed the bridges. He had all the boats on the Severn removed and spoiled the fords by dredging to make them too deep for crossing. Thus de Montfort was trapped on the far side of the river and the prince was able to take his time.

De Montfort sent a messenger to young Simon de Montfort telling him to raise the siege of Pevensey Castle and to go to their castle at Kenilworth with as large a force as he could raise. De Montfort knew that the prince's army was dangerously large, and he wanted to have his son's army as well, to be as strong as possible before they came to battle. By the 31st July, 1265, the three armies were close together, Prince Edward at Worcester, de Montfort at Hereford, twenty-seven miles away, and young

Simon de Montfort at Kenilworth, thirty-four miles from Worcester.

Simon de Montfort was still on the other side of the Severn, and Prince Edward decided to deal with de Montfort the younger at Kenilworth first. It was essential to his success, of course, to prevent the two de Montfort armies joining forces. He had ideas of his own about warfare, which asked much of his men. That they never failed him is sure proof of his excellence as a general.

On the evening of the 1st August, Edward paraded his army in Worcester – it seems to have been about ten thousand strong – and led them on the thirty-four-mile night march to Kenilworth. As they drew near before dawn, his scouts hurried back to report that they had heard the sound of a moving multitude. It seemed that young de Montfort had been told of his approach and was preparing to meet him. Edward marched on and found that the noise was caused by a convoy of baggage wagons taking food and supplies to Kenilworth. He attacked the convoy with such vigour that not a single man was able to get away to warn young de Montfort. The food was taken from the wagons to provide a welcome breakfast for the prince's army, and the march was continued to Kenilworth.

Young de Montfort's army was taken completely unawares. Most of the army, including de Montfort, were encamped or billeted in houses outside the castle. With no warning, they were suddenly set upon by the royalist soldiers, who rushed through the town, yelling in triumph and cutting down the sleepy enemy as they stumbled out of tents and houses. The prince's men swept right up to the walls of the castle. Nearly all the barons with young Simon fell into their hands without being able to resist. Young Simon de Montfort himself escaped into the castle, half dressed from his bed, and the portcullis was quickly lowered and the drawbridge raised. Many barons and knights were actually captured in their beds. The only survivors were those who had slept inside the castle. It was a brilliant and devastating stroke.

Prisoners and booty were secured, and thirteen banners; but there was to be no rest for the victors. The prince gathered together his men, added his prisoners to the column, took fresh horses, and within a couple of hours set off on the thirty-four-mile march back to Worcester.

It is a tribute to his leadership that it was possible. Late that evening Prince Edward led his weary but triumphant army into Worcester. The soldiers must have looked forward to well-deserved rest; they had marched sixty-eight miles and utterly defeated the enemy, all within twenty-four hours. But under their vigorous young commander there was to be little rest for them yet.

In Worcester Prince Edward received important news. Before he left for Kenilworth the night before, he had withdrawn his patrols along the River Severn, needing every available man for his attack on Kenilworth. While he was away, Simon de Montfort had crossed the Severn at Kempsey, four miles south of Worcester, and was encamped not far off. A number of unlucky soldiers were called up from their billets for sentry duty, while the rest of the prince's army slept.

In the morning, Prince Edward learnt that de Montfort was marching westwards, apparently to cross the River Avon at Pershore. It was clear that de Montfort was marching towards Kenilworth to join up with his son, knowing nothing of the disaster that had befallen him. De Montfort's route towards Kenilworth would be through Evesham, and then either through Alcester or Stratford-on-Avon. The prince saw what he must do – march westwards at once to cut the Evesham–Alcester and the Evesham–Stratford roads. So Prince Edward's army were called on parade in the afternoon of the 3rd August to make yet another night march, this time of twenty miles.

The prince formed his army into three columns, one commanded by himself, one by Gloucester and the third by Mortimer. They left Worcester in the early evening and struck the Evesham–Alcester road three miles south of Alcester. De Montfort was still at Evesham. The prince separated his three columns. He sent the Earl of Gloucester directly down the road to Evesham with orders to take up a strong defensive position north of the town.

Mortimer's column was sent southwards as well, to march round Evesham to come up behind the town and so close de Montfort's line of retreat across the bridge over the Avon. The prince himself led his column in a south-easterly direction to the Evesham–Stratford-on-Avon road, to meet de Montfort if he should leave Evesham by that route. It will be noted that, being a good commander, the prince himself undertook the longest march of the three.

Prince Edward crossed the River Avon at Cleve Prior, and, after an hour's march towards Evesham, crossed the river again at a bridge at Offenham, a little over a mile north-east of Evesham.

Simon de Montfort, with the king and his small court, was billeted in the priory at Evesham. At dawn on the 4th August de Montfort received news that a scout on the priory bell-tower had sighted a strong column of armed men marching from Offenham bridge, and at the head of the column were the banners of young de Montfort and twelve of the barons with him at Kenilworth. It seemed that the two de Montfort armies were to be united, and father and son would fight together with sufficient force to vanquish the royal rebel. Then the truth was realised: the column was Prince Edward's, the banners the spoils of his victory at Kenilworth.

Worse news was to follow. Scouts reported that the Earl of Gloucester was in battle array across the road northwards out of Evesham, and Edward was joining him. On top of this came the final news, which spelt disaster for de Montfort. Roger Mortimer had come up south of Evesham with a third column and had captured the only bridge across the Severn, barring retreat southwards. De Montfort was trapped. The River Avon loops closely round Evesham, leaving only a one-thousand-five-hundred-yard gap to the north. That gap was closed by the prince and Gloucester, and Mortimer stopped retreat to the south.

The fifty-seven-year-old warrior, who had campaigned brilliantly in France and Germany, who had won a great reputation in the Holy Land as a Crusader, and who was victor at Lewes fifteen months before, was completely out-generalled by the twenty-six-year-old prince. Prince Edward had destroyed half the enemy's force; now his swift night-march and the brilliant deployment of his army had trapped de Montfort. The prince stood on commanding high ground north of Evesham with ten thousand men to the enemy's five thousand. 'May God have mercy on our souls,' de Montfort said, 'for our bodies are theirs!'

He is said to have given the barons with him permission to save themselves if they could. They refused, choosing to fight it out to the death. Surrender does not seem to have been considered. De Montfort knew that the prince must have extended his line to cover as much of the one-thousand-five-hundred-yard gap as possible. In this he saw a ray of hope. The traditional method of advancing to battle was in line of three divisions abreast. Instead of this he formed his army in column, on a narrow front, to try to smash his way through the thin line by sheer weight of numbers. Once through he might be able to hold the enemy back with a rearguard action while the main column marched hard for Kenilworth Castle.

The small army was marshalled accordingly, the mounted knights first, about sixty horses abreast; behind them were the English foot soldiers, and the Welsh foot soldiers brought up the rear. King Henry was made to ride behind the knights, in full armour. As the army was forming up at nine o'clock in the morning of the 4th August, 1265, a violent thunderstorm broke. The king was frightened, for he was a timorous old gentleman. It must have been an unnerving experience for the boldest, to be in a thunderstorm, with vivid lightning, when you were encased in steel armour.

When de Montfort's five thousand were ready, and the summer storm was rumbling away into the distance, the banners were raised, trumpets sounded and they marched up the mile-long hill out of Evesham. On the hill the prince's banners were flying too, a brave line of fluttering colour, with the royal banner beside Prince Edward, and the red chevrons of de Clare flying above Gloucester. It was a dramatic moment. Prince Edward awaited his foe, proud of the success of his strategy, proud of the long hard marches his men had made; proud, too, to be fighting to rescue his father.

De Montfort, great and seasoned warrior, must have found a grim relish in the situation, for he was a fighting man and soon he would be fighting as never before, against heavy, almost hopeless odds. The barons and knights shared de Montfort's fierce determination to dare all, for they were fighting men, born and bred.

The Welsh foot soldiers had a different view of the situation. They were prepared to fight and risk death in a reasonable battle, with a fair chance of victory, which had always gone to de Montfort's men. But this was different, and the quarrel, after all, was none of theirs. Gradually at first, and then in greater numbers, they fell out of the ranks and slipped away into the fields and gardens alongside the road, and then over the fields to the river. Only a few escaped, for Mortimer's men at the south of the town saw them trying to escape and hunted them down. They hauled them out of houses, dragged them from ditches and hedges and slew them. Many of those who swam the river were cut down on the other side.

De Montfort's column marched steadily up the hill, a solid mass of three thousand five hundred which is, when you consider it, a formidable array. Swords were drawn, lances at the ready, pikes at the trail. They marched straight for the centre of the prince's line and attacked with such weight and fury that the line, probably only three or four deep, inevitably gave. It gave but it did not break, and as the long column fought into the line, the two wings of the princes' army advanced, wheeling left and right to attack the flanks of the column. As the wheeling movement developed, de Montfort's column was encircled.

There was no escape for de Montfort's men, no mercy was asked or given. De Montfort's barons, knights and foot soldiers faced outwards as the circle enclosed about them. De Montfort's eldest son fell mortally wounded, and de Montfort himself was unhorsed. 'Is my son slain?' he is said to have asked. 'Then it is time for me to die!' He took his sword in both hands and strode forward, clumsy in full armour, into the thickest of the fight. Half

Simon de Montfort at the Battle of Evesham, 1265

a dozen royalist knights attacked him, eager for the honour of killing the famous soldier. De Montfort swung his sword in magnificent desperation, the lion at bay. At last a sword found a gap in the back of his armour and he fell.

His friends died fighting round his corpse, half the greatest names in the land. In the midst of the throng was King Henry III, the pious man of peace taken there against his will. Some royalist soldiers came upon him and attacked him. The old king raised his visor. 'Know you not me?' he said. 'I am Henry of Winchester, your king!'

The battle ended only when more than half de Montfort's men had been slain. The victory was complete. The old poet, Robert of Gloucester, wrote: 'Such was the murder of Evesham, for battle it was none.'

Murderous it certainly was. An estimate of de Montfort's casualties given at the time shows his losses as one hundred and eighty knights, two hundred and twenty squires, and two thousand foot soldiers, while the royalists lost no more than a handful of knights. These figures may well be reasonably accurate. The completeness of the victory was the direct result of the prince's generalship, bringing his enemy to battle in conditions which gave him every advantage.

Thus Prince Edward rescued his father, and the royal authority was re-established. The life of Simon de Montfort was not in vain. He had fought and died for a principle which was to be continuously in the minds and hearts of Englishmen. The Parliament he created, with elected representatives privileged to criticise the government, set the pattern for parliamentary government the world over, though many centuries were to pass before the principle for which he died was finally established. The battle of Evesham was, in a way, the prelude to the Civil War of 1642. It was also a battle between two great soldiers, in which the younger showed his mastery of strategy, and the older how a brave man can die.

Chapter 4

Robert the Bruce Frees Scotland

The Battle of Bannockburn

24th June 1314

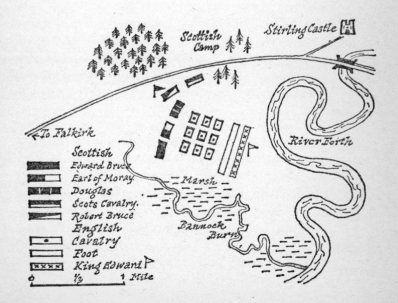

King Edward I, victor of the battle of Evesham and successor to his father King Henry III, dreamed of ruling over a united kingdom of England, Wales and Scotland. He achieved half of his ambition when, after a brilliant five-year campaign, he conquered Wales in 1282. Nine years later he became the overlord of the king of Scotland, but by consent and not by conquest.

The circumstances which brought about this sovereignty over Scotland arose from the death of King Alexander III of Scotland in 1286. His heir was his granddaughter Margaret, the daughter of the King of Norway. The princess, the 'Maid of Norway', was only three years old but the Scottish nobles recognised her succession as Queen of Scots, and the country was governed by a regency in her name, while she lived with her parents in Norway.

When Margaret was six an arrangement was made between Scotland and England which fitted well with King Edward's plans. The six-year-old Queen was affianced to King Edward's eldest son, also named Edward and then aged seven. By this means, when Prince Edward grew up he would be the husband of the queen of Scotland, a short step to becoming king of Scotland, and the dream of a united kingdom would come true.

When she was seven the Maid of Norway was sent to England to meet Prince Edward. She sailed from Bergen in royal state, but in the Orkneys she was taken mysteriously ill and died. Thus King Edward's plans came to nought.

There was now no obvious heir to the throne of Scotland, and three nobles had what seemed to be equal claims. Rather than plunge Scotland into civil war, they asked the king of England to decide which should be king, promising to abide by his decision.

King Edward agreed, provided whoever was chosen should swear fealty to him as his overlord. The conditions were accepted and a special court considered the claims of the three men and reported their findings to King Edward. He announced that the new king of Scotland was John de Baliol. Baliol swore fealty to King Edward, and was crowned at Scone. Thus easily did Edward become overlord of Scotland, a situation which could not endure with a race as proud as the Scots.

Within three years Baliol revolted against King Edward, and declared Scotland free and independent, and no vassal State. Edward I was a man of action. He promptly raised an army and invaded Scotland to enforce his sovereignty. He met with little resistance, for the Scottish nobles were divided among themselves.

A Scottish army was defeated at Dunbar, where three hundred and fifty years later Oliver Cromwell was to defeat another Scottish army which was fighting for Charles II of England. Edward took a cruel vengeance, massacring and burning, and engendering thereby a great hatred for the English in Scottish hearts. King Baliol surrendered and was taken south to the Tower of London. Edward destroyed the Great Seal of Scotland, and took away all the national records and the Stone of Scone, on which the kings of Scotland were crowned. He made a triumphal march through Scotland, and garrisoned the main castles to keep the country in subjection.

Neither fear of Edward's vengeance, nor the presence of the English garrisons could keep the Scots in subjection. Two patriots came to the fore, to lead Scotland against the English – William

Wallace and Robert Bruce, names which are immortalised in Robert Burns's proud song:

> *Scots, wha hae wi' Wallace bled,*
> *Scots, wham Bruce has aften led,*
> *Welcome to your gory bed*
> *Or to victory!*
>
> *Now's the day and now's the hour;*
> *See the front o' battle lour,*
> *See approach proud Edward's power –*
> *Chains and slavery!*

When Sir William Wallace, the son of a small land-owner, took arms against the English, Scotsmen from every part of the land hastened to join him. He quickly found himself at the head of an army – 'The Army of the Commons of Scotland'. In 1297 Wallace utterly defeated an English army at Cambuskenneth. In 1298 Edward marched north again, to restore his authority in his vassal kingdom, and defeated Wallace at the battle of Falkirk. It was a crushing defeat, but it did nothing to curb the spirit of rebellion, and Wallace himself escaped capture.

Wallace continued his romantic and gallant opposition until he was at last captured in 1305, and executed for treason. Outwardly Scotland was subdued, but inwardly she was boiling with resentment and ready for any action which might help to overthrow the English. A new leader was ready, Robert the Bruce, grandson of one of the claimants to the crown of Scotland in 1291. The leadership of Bruce was confirmed when he was crowned King Robert I of Scotland in 1306. Within three months he met an English army at Methven, near Perth, and suffered defeat.

Misfortune crowded on the new king of Scotland, and he spent the winter of 1306–7 as a fugitive, hiding in the lonely island of Rachrine, off the north coast of Ireland. He had been defeated, two of his brothers had been captured and executed, he was excommunicated and outlawed, a king with no kingdom. The adventures of Robert Bruce can be read in Sir Walter Scott's great novels, *Lord of the Isles* and *Tales of a Grandfather*. There are many legends about Bruce, the most famous being the story of the spider, whose determination and patience were said to inspire him to continue the struggle, hopeless though it seemed.

Robert Bruce returned to Scotland, raised another army, and met the English again, at Loudon, and this time he won. The great test lay ahead, however, for King Edward was marching north yet again. But he did not reach Scotland, for at Burgh-on-the-Sands, near Carlisle, King Edward I, 'the Hammer of the Scots' died, his ambition of ruling Scotland unfulfilled.

The new king of England, Edward II, had little of his father's strength and determination. He was more artist than warrior, a charming but luxurious young man. He ignored Scotland for seven years, so that Robert Bruce was able to make raids deep into England, and to expel the English garrisons from Scottish castles one by one. In 1310 Edward II made an effort to act like his father and raised an army and invaded Scotland, but it was a half-hearted affair. Bruce preferred his successful guerrilla tactics, and avoided battle, and soon Edward marched south again, his efforts wasted.

By 1314 only Stirling Castle, the most vital of all, remained in English hands. It was so closely besieged by Robert Bruce that the governor sent word to Edward II that unless he was rescued by midsummer day he would be forced to surrender. This goaded Edward II and his friends into action. Elaborate arrangements were made to summon troops from all England, and even from France and Germany. Ships were sent to Ireland for soldiers. Edward intended to take such an immense army to Scotland that even Robert Bruce would be daunted, and victory certain.

When King Edward marched north he commanded twenty thousand infantry and three thousand cavalry. A great number of wagons went with the army, too, because the English knights, following the example of their luxurious king, intended to make war in comfort. Robert Bruce made no attempt to prevent the English crossing the border into Scotland. He had only ten thousand men and he wanted to fight on ground of his own choosing. The country north of the border was laid waste, so that the enemy could not find food, and Bruce waited for it near Stirling, by a stream called Bannockburn.

The position was two and a half miles south of Stirling; a plateau protected on one side by the marshy ground on each side of Bannockburn, and on the other by woodland. It was a clever place to make a stand, because the large English army would be crowded together on a narrow front between the marsh and the woods with little room for manoeuvre.

The advance guard of the English army came to Bannockburn on the 23rd June, and halted to await the main army. A body of English led by Sir Henry Bohun advanced up the main road towards Stirling, intending to communicate with the governor of the castle. Riding up the road, Bohun suddenly found himself facing the Scottish army. At the head was the king of Scotland, wearing the crown. Bohun put his lance at the ready and charged straight at the king in a gallant attempt to end the war with one blow. Robert Bruce was mounted on a riding horse, not on his war horse, which was trained for battle. But he took his battle-axe from his saddlebow and stood fast. As Bohun charged down on him, Robert Bruce deftly turned the lance aside with his axe and then, with a swift powerful blow at the back of Bohun's helmet, brained his adversary. Their leader killed, the English turned about and hurried away. This sudden single combat in the presence of the army between the English knight and Robert Bruce is a cherished memory of the great Scottish hero.

During the night the whole English army came up and prepared to form up into their battle array. Bruce had expected them to attack from the south, on the direct road to Stirling. But the English scouts recommended an attack from the north-east, where the ground was firmer for the large number of cavalry. Accordingly they marched past the Scottish position on its eastern side, wheeled and got ready to attack in a south-westerly direction.

The Scots therefore changed their front, to face north-east. Bruce had his ten thousand foot soldiers in four divisions. The division on the right was commanded by his younger brother,

Single combat between Sir Henry Bohun and Robert Bruce, 1314

Edward; the Earl of Moray commanded the centre, and James Douglas the left. Bruce himself commanded the fourth division, holding it in reserve on the left, with his small cavalry contingent of five hundred picked men, under Sir Robert Keith, the Marshal of Scotland.

Dawn of Midsummer Day, 24th June, 1314, found both armies perfecting their positions. The English cavalry was organised into ten divisions, in three lines of three battles each, with the tenth as advance guard, forward and to the left of the line, commanded by the Earl of Gloucester. The English infantry was massed in two dense lines behind the cavalry. King Edward II was in the rear with his personal bodyguard of five hundred knights.

The smaller Scottish army, which had been in the position for several days, was in battle order long before the English were ready, and Bruce decided to take the initiative and attack at once before the English were ready. Thus it was that while the English were still marching and countermarching into their positions crowded together on a narrow front, three of the Scottish divisions appeared from the woodland where they had been hidden and marched quickly downhill, pikes ready.

The first to engage was Edward Bruce, on the right, meeting Gloucester's advance guard of the English cavalry, who charged to meet them. There was an immediate clash of foot soldier versus horseman, pike against lance and sword. In the words of an old chronicler,

> The two hosts came together, and the great steeds of the knights dashed into the Scottish pikes as into a thick wood; there arose a great and horrible crash from rending lances and dying horses, and they stood locked together for a space.

The awe-inspiring charge of the knights had failed to break the Scottish ranks. Locked in battle, fighting at thrust of pike and lance, English knights and Scottish pikemen strove to drive each other back. The knights withdrew and charged again, but to no effect, and gradually they were borne back.

While this furious fighting continued on the Scottish right, the three divisions of English horse in the front line hastened to get into position to receive the other two divisions of Scottish pike-men hurrying down the hill towards them. Some English archers on the right were led forward quickly to the front, and tried to break the Scottish advance with flights of swiftly shot arrows. 'The English shot so fast that, if only their shooting had lasted, it would have been hard for the Scots,' wrote the Scottish poet John Barbour, who talked with many who had fought at Bannockburn.

The situation was saved by Keith's five hundred horsemen, which Bruce had posted on the left flank for just such a purpose as this. Keith charged the English archers, and scattered and slew them, reining in his men when the task was done to ride back to the flank again, ready for another emergency. Such skilful control of charging cavalry was a rare quality in battle.

When the English archers were driven off, Moray and Douglas led their pikemen at the dense body of English horse. Barbour wrote: 'Whether it was through the narrowness of the front they were fighting upon, or whether from demoralisation, I know not; but it seemed they were all one mass.' Against this mass the Scottish pikemen threw themselves, thrusting at horses and riders.

The pile of dead and dying horses and men mounted. The English fought furiously, with no thought of retreat. Behind them the rest of the cavalry and the massed infantry were helpless, cramped close together on the narrow front. The English archers and spearmen had to wait helpless while the cavalry were fighting a losing battle in front of them. The archers tried to help by shooting high, hoping the arrows would fall only on the Scots. But according to a chronicler, 'They hit some few Scots in the breast, but struck many more English in the back.'

While the front line of the English army and the three divisions of Scots were locked in a general and furious mêlée, Robert Bruce suddenly led his fourth division of pikemen forward. This onslaught of fresh men, led by the great Scottish hero himself, turned the tide of battle. The mass of English cavalry tried to fall back, trapped though they were by the hosts behind them. In the rear the English foot began to melt away, and then occurred a strange incident.

The Scottish camp followers – camp guards, servants, grooms and such-like – had been watching the battle from the hill-top. Seeing the mighty English army begin to give, they gathered up what weapons they could, tied coloured cloths on sticks to look like banners, and ran down the hill, blowing horns and shouting, 'Slay! Slay!' When the English saw them, several thousand in number, they imagined it was yet another Scottish reserve, and the infantry turned and hurried away, and the retreat became general. King Edward wheeled his horse and galloped off with his five hundred knights.

The last to turn away were the men in front. Their officers were nearly all slain, they had fought hard and bravely, but it had been impossible to prevail against the men of Robert Bruce. Turning their backs on the hideous rampart of dead and dying men and horses, they galloped away.

The battle of Bannockburn was the worst defeat ever suffered by an English army, and they had taken the field with twenty-three thousand men against ten thousand. There is no figure of the total English casualties, but the dead included the Earl of Gloucester, forty-two barons, and, according to Barbour, two hundred knights and seven hundred esquires. The Earl of Hereford, twenty-two barons and sixty-eight knights were taken prisoner. The Scots lost only two knights, but a great number of pikemen.

The disgraced English army straggled towards the border, hunted and murdered by the Scottish peasants. Stirling Castle surrendered, and Scotland was free of English rule, freed by Robert the Bruce and his small but unconquerable army.

Chapter 5

Red Rose and White Rose

The Battles of St Albans

22nd May 1455

and

17th February 1461

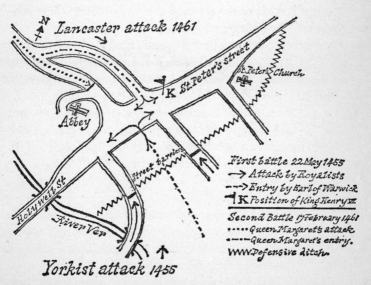

Lancaster attack 1461

St Peter's street

K St. Peter's street

St. Peter's Church

Abbey

Street barriers

Holy well St.

River Ver

Yorkist attack 1455

First battle 22 May 1455
→ Attack by Royalists
---→ Entry by Earl of Warwick
K Position of King Henry VI

Second Battle 17 February 1461
••••• Queen Margaret's attack
-•-•- Queen Margaret's entry
WWW Defensive ditch

The first Battle of St Albans in 1455 began the Wars of the Roses, a pretty name for thirty years of ugly warfare. The war was fought between two branches of the royal family of England, the Plantagenets, who had ruled England for three centuries. At the beginning of the war Henry VI was king, the descendant of John of Gaunt, Duke of Lancaster. His rival was his kinsman, Richard, Duke of York, descended from Edmund, Duke of York. To understand the Wars of the Roses it is essential to get these relations clear, and the table on pages 60–61 will help in that.

The struggle for the crown of England lasted thirty years, from 1455 to 1485. It was fought between the two royal houses of Lancaster and York. The badge of Lancaster was the red rose, of York the white rose – hence the Wars of the Roses.

Before the wars ended about seven out of ten of the great nobles of the land were killed – slain in battle, murdered or executed. Something like a hundred thousand English soldiers died. Never have there been such fierce and murderous battles as the fourteen fought between Lancaster and York, the red rose and the white.

The long war can be better understood if we break the battles up into two campaigns. One battle is the prelude, two provide an interlude, and Bosworth in 1485 is the grand finale. This list shows that the two main campaigns both lasted two years.

You will see that York won ten battles to Lancaster's four.

After the battle of Tewkesbury in 1471, York held their victory for fourteen years; but Lancaster won the last battle and that is the one that counts. We are going to look at four of these battles: the two at St Albans, Towton, and, most important of them all, Bosworth.

	Date	Battle	Victor
Prelude	1455 (May)	St Albans	York
First Campaign	1459 (September)	Blore Heath, near Market Drayton, Shropshire	York
	1460 (July)	Northampton	York
	1460 (December)	Wakefield, Yorkshire	Lancaster
	1461 (February)	Mortimer's Cross, near Leominster, Herefordshire	York
	1461 (February)	St Albans	Lancaster
	1461 (March)	Towton, Northumberland	York
Interlude	1464 (April)	Hedgeley Moor, near Wooler, Northumberland	York
	1464 (May)	Hexham, Northumberland	York
Second Campaign	1469 (July)	Banbury	Lancaster
	1470 (March)	Stamford	York
	1471 (April)	Barnet	York
	1471 (May)	Tewkesbury	York
Final Battle	1485 (August)	Bosworth, near Leicester	Lancaster

The confusion of persons and events can be untangled by following the story of one small family, a man, his wife and their young son, the family whose fortunes were most concerned. The man is King Henry VI, head of the house of Lancaster and son of the hero King Henry V, victor of Agincourt. But Henry VI was no hero. He was a dreamer, a gentle, trusting person, ill-suited to rule the hot-blooded English in the age into which he was born. Henry VI succeeded to the crown when he was one year old. He was, we are told, a mild, good and honest boy, educated by carefully chosen nurses and teachers who were instructed to use 'reasonable chastisement' when necessary. Henry was crowned in 1429, when he was seven years old, and he was such a serious and studious boy that he opened Parliament himself when he was ten.

Henry VI grew up into a man of peace, kindly and very religious. He would have been happy living as a scholar in the peace of a monastery. Instead it was his destiny to rule an England which, under Edward I, Edward III and Henry V, had become the most formidable and war-like nation in Europe, the nation which had crushed the French at Crécy, Poitiers and Agincourt. The greatest pride of Henry VI was not battles, but the foundation of Eton and King's College, Cambridge, and, in the name of his wife, Queens' College, Cambridge.

Henry married Margaret of Anjou, daughter of the Duke of Anjou, a queen as forceful as the king was gentle, and as cruel to her enemies as he was tender-hearted. When the realm was torn by civil war, Queen Margaret took vigorous action on behalf of her husband, raised armies and led them in the field, never giving up even when the cause of Lancaster seemed quite hopeless. She fought to the end, to save her husband's kingdom and the inheritance of their son, Edward, Prince of Wales. When the Wars of the Roses began, it was only twenty-five years since Joan of Arc had saved the French army in the war with England. Joan the Maid was a great French heroine, and it seems that Queen Margaret, a French woman, saw herself as a second Joan, sent by God to save the king of England from his enemies.

The third member of this tragic royal family was Edward, Prince of Wales, son of the mild father and the aggressive mother. He was born in 1453, two years before the Wars of the Roses began. He had a wretched childhood, with none of the tranquillity his father had enjoyed. The little boy was hurried from castle to castle, often having to flee from pursuing enemies. He grew up in an atmosphere of strain and battle. The little education he was able to receive was directed towards making him a warrior, fit to rule the battle-torn realm he would inherit.

King Henry VI, Queen Margaret and Edward, Prince of Wales, were the centre of the Wars of the Roses. To them rallied all who supported the house of Lancaster, the red rose. Against them were arrayed the supporters of Richard, Duke of York, and, after his death, of his son, Edward, Earl of March, the side of the white rose.

Before Prince Edward was born Richard of York was heir to the throne. As the family tree on pages 60–61 shows, York's claim to the throne was as strong as Henry's; in some ways it could be considered stronger. Both were descended from sons of King Edward III. Henry VI was the great-grandson of John of Gaunt, the fourth son of Edward III. The Duke of York was the grandson of Edmund Langley, Edward III's fifth son. York was also descended, through his mother, from Lionel, Duke of Clarence, Edward III's third son. You will also see from the table that Henry VI's grandfather, Henry IV , had usurped the throne from his cousin, King Richard II. These three facts gave the Duke of York a strong claim to the crown.

York, with most other Englishmen, was outraged when, piece by piece, English provinces in France were given up by King Henry. Englishmen whose fathers and grandfathers had fought to keep these rich provinces despised the king who surrendered them weakly.

When the king was thirty-two years old, in 1453, he was stricken with a severe mental illness. He lived in a strange mad world of his own, recognising no one. The Duke of York took over the government, and governed well. The king recovered, after fifteen months, and unwisely dismissed the Duke of York from the office of chief minister and appointed York's enemy, the Duke of Somerset.

The Duke of York went off in a rage to his own lands in the north of England. After governing the country admirably he had

Wars of the Roses
Simplified Table of the Houses of Plantagenet and Tudor

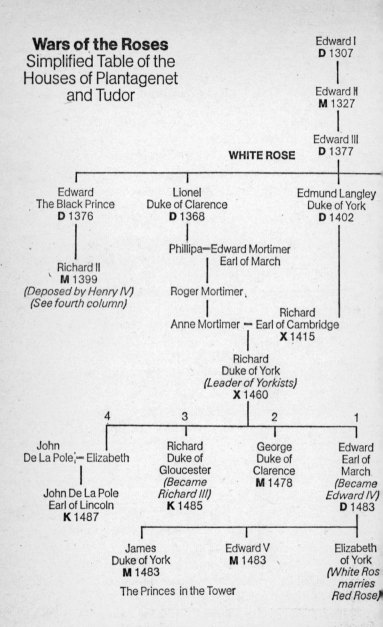

Edward I
D 1307

Edward II
M 1327

Edward III
D 1377

WHITE ROSE

Edward
The Black Prince
D 1376

Lionel
Duke of Clarence
D 1368

Edmund Langley
Duke of York
D 1402

Richard II
M 1399
(Deposed by Henry IV)
(See fourth column)

Phillipa━Edward Mortimer
Earl of March

Roger Mortimer

Anne Mortimer ━ Richard
Earl of Cambridge
X 1415

Richard
Duke of York
(Leader of Yorkists)
X 1460

4

3

2

1

John
De La Pole━Elizabeth

Richard
Duke of
Gloucester
*(Became
Richard III)*
K 1485

George
Duke of
Clarence
M 1478

Edward
Earl of
March
*(Became
Edward IV)*
D 1483

John De La Pole
Earl of Lincoln
K 1487

James
Duke of York
M 1483

Edward V
M 1483

Elizabeth
of York
*(White Ros
marries
Red Rose)*

The Princes in the Tower

D = Died   K = Killed in battle
M = Murdered   X = Executed

RED ROSE

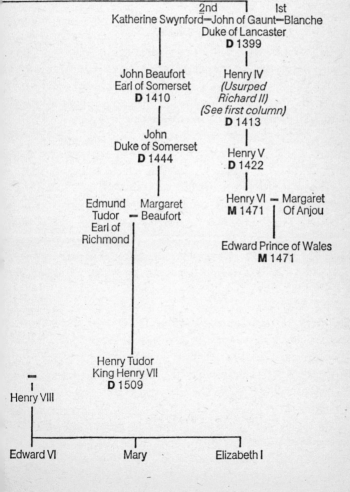

2nd
Katherine Swynford═John of Gaunt═Blanche
Duke of Lancaster
D 1399
1st

John Beaufort
Earl of Somerset
D 1410

Henry IV
*(Usurped
Richard II)
(See first column)*
D 1413

John
Duke of Somerset
D 1444

Henry V
D 1422

Edmund
Tudor — Margaret
Earl of   Beaufort
Richmond

Henry VI — Margaret
M 1471   Of Anjou

Edward Prince of Wales
M 1471

Henry Tudor
King Henry VII
D 1509

Henry VIII

Edward VI   Mary   Elizabeth I

61

been dismissed and replaced by his enemy Somerset. A prince had been born, and so York was removed from the succession to the throne. York summoned his friends to take up arms. The Earl of Salisbury joined him, and so did the Earl of Warwick, later to be known as Warwick the Kingmaker. Each one took with him a large number of knights. A powerful army was formed with its badge the white rose of York. The Duke of Somerset and other barons who supported the king summoned their armed men, to resist the Yorkist insurrection.

If you had been living in 1455 you would have found yourself thinking in one of three ways about this quarrel between the Lancaster king and the Duke of York. You might have said, 'The king is a good man, son of the great Henry V. He has been our king since he was one year old. He was annointed and crowned, and whatever his faults I am his man.' On the other hand, you might have said, 'The king may be good, but he is too weak to rule England. Under him we have lost our conquests in France. The Duke of York has an equal, or better, claim to the crown. He is a strong man and a born leader. I am for York.' It might have been, however, that you would have said, 'I've got plenty to do looking after my farm – or my shop. These quarrels between the great ones don't concern me. I'm going to mind my own business and keep out of it.' In that case – and there would have been many like you – you would have gone about your own business hoping that if civil war did come no battles would be fought in your neighbourhood.

The two armies were no amateur forces. In the past century Englishmen had been bred to war. The barons and knights were skilled in fighting and each had his armour ready in his hall. There was also a magnificent tradition among the ordinary Englishmen in archery, and nearly every man had in his chimney corner his well cared-for longbow.

The longbow had come into use in England in the reign of Edward I, who had rescued his father at the battle of Evesham. In his long campaign in Wales Edward I had seen what a powerful weapon the Welshman's longbow was. The bows used previously were short weapons used at close range, and the more popular form was the crossbow, a mechanical device usually firing iron bolts. But the English longbow was quite different. It was made of carefully chosen wood, six feet long, and shooting an arrow a yard long. Used with strength and skill it could shoot an arrow which would pierce plate armour at two hundred and fifty yards.

It was the highly skilled English bowmen who made the victories in France possible. Every man between the age of sixteen and sixty was bound by law to possess and practise the longbow. Archery was a compulsory sport, and Englishmen practised regularly at the butts in town or village. A man could be sent to prison for not practising with his bow and playing 'handball, football or hockey, coursing and cock-fighting, or such other games'.

Boys were carefully trained as bowmen, and looked forward to the day when they could shoot with the men at the butts. In the sixteenth century, Bishop Latimer told how his father taught him to use the longbow.

> He taught me to draw, how to lay my body in my bow, and not to draw with strength of arms as other nations do, but with strength of the body. I had my bows bought me according to my age and strength; as I increased in them, so my bows were made bigger and bigger. For men shall never shoot well unless they be brought up in it.

Thus the knights and bowmen who rallied to the house of York or Lancaster in 1455 were highly skilled in the art of war. That is one reason why there were such terrible losses on both sides in the battles of the Wars of the Roses. Another reason was the hatred which was engendered, and the long tale of vengeance.

At the beginning of May the Duke of York marched down the Great North Road at the head of some three thousand men. The knights were the officers, and the rank and file were the bowmen and the billmen – foot soldiers armed with a bill or spear. The Duke was careful not to say that he was in arms against the king. His purpose was to remove the men he considered to be the king's evil councillors, meaning particularly his enemy, the Duke of

Somerset. This was made clear so that he and his men could not be accused of treason. King Henry VI marched north from London with an army, also about three thousand strong, to meet the Duke of York. The king did not want to meet him too near London, which was dangerously sympathetic to the Duke of York.

York's army was at Royston, forty miles north of London, when the royal army left London. St Albans was half-way between them, and both armies marched hard to get there first. The king just won the race, entering St Albans early in the morning of the 22nd May. At the same time, the Duke of York halted his army in the fields outside the city.

Both sides paused, hoping to negotiate a peace. The king sent the Duke of Buckingham to talk things over with the Duke of York. Buckingham came back with a courteous message that York would take his army back to the north of England if the king would hand over the Duke of Somerset to be executed. The king, always faithful to his friends, is said to have exclaimed, 'By the faith I owe to St Edward and to the Crown of England, I shall destroy them, every mother's son, and they shall be hanged, and drawn and quartered.' Both armies prepared to battle, the Duke of York to attack St Albans and the king to defend it.

St Albans was then a small town clustered round its abbey. It was not walled, but there was a ditch, and barriers could be lowered across the streets.

York attacked with two columns, advancing up Sopwell Lane and Shropshire Lane, both of which led to the main street, to be stopped at the barriers. A brisk and deadly duel developed between the archers, but no progress could be made into the town. Richard Neville, the twenty-five-year-old Earl of Warwick, solved the problem. He found a place between Sopwell Lane and Shropshire Lane where the defensive ditch could be crossed unobserved, because of the houses and gardens.

Warwick led his column across the ditch, and his men knocked holes in the back of the houses which confronted them. Warwick then led his men through the houses, out of the front doors, and into the main street, 'blowing up his trumpets and shouting with a great voice, "A Warwick! A Warwick!" ' The column came into the main street of St Albans opposite the abbey, and neatly split the king's forces into two.

With the Yorkists between and behind the two blocks of royalist defenders, the battle became fast and furious. The defenders had to leave the barricades to deal with the attack in their rear, so that the other two Yorkist columns could fight their way up Sopwell Lane and Shropshire Lane into the main street. Arrows shot by experts from longbows at close range wrought terrible destruction in the confined space of St Peters Street and Hollywell Street. As the Yorkist bowmen drove back the enemy, the knights, heavily armoured and fighting on foot, closed with the Lancaster knights. The Abbot of St Albans was watching; he wrote, 'Here you saw one fall with his brains dashed out, there another with a broken arm, a third with a cut throat, and a fourth with a pierced chest, and the whole street was full of dead corpses.'

The Yorkists, having split the enemy, had the advantage, but the king's men fought back stubbornly. King Henry VI did not take part in the battle; he sat on a chair under a tree, where the royal standard had been set up at the southern end of St Peters Street, now the market place.

The Yorkists gradually approached the royal standard. The king was wounded by an arrow; the standard bearer threw down the standard and ran for his life, and suddenly it was over. The king was almost alone, surrounded by his enemies, and bleeding from the wound in his neck. The Duke of York came up and knelt before him, to ask his forgiveness. He declared that he was in all things his man. The king was escorted to the Abbey with all due reverence.

The object of the battle had been to remove the Duke of Somerset from his position as chief councillor to the king. That object was achieved, for Somerset was killed in the battle. The Duke of York led his victorious troops to London, escorting the king in state. For the next four years, although the king seemed to rule, the Duke of York was the master of England.

King Henry may have been reconciled to the new state of affairs, in which he was left in peace to follow his own pursuits while York and his friends ruled the country, but Queen Margaret could not accept it. She hated the Duke of York and tried in every way to undermine his power. She was determined to free the king, and, most important to her, to clear the succession for her baby prince. The conflict between the Duke of York and the queen reached a climax four years after St Albans, when the queen's friends raised an army in the west of England, where the supporters of Lancaster were thickest. But the queen's army was defeated by the Yorkists at the battle of Blore Heath, near Market Drayton in Shropshire.

The queen was undaunted. She raised another army, and the next year she was herself present, with the seven-year-old prince, at the battle of Northampton. Again the Yorkists, under the Earl of Warwick, were victorious. The queen fled from the field of battle with the prince, and after a number of alarming adventures reached the safety of Harlech Castle. From Harlech the queen and the prince got safely to Scotland. Here, in spite of having suffered two sound defeats, this extraordinary woman set about raising another army.

The Duke of York, exasperated by the queen's stubborn resistance, 'persuaded' Parliament to name him as the heir to the throne. The king had to approve, and so disinherited his son. Queen Margaret's rage at this news can be imagined.

Queen Margaret soon acted, and led a very large army of English and Scottish troops over the border into England. She met the army of the Duke of York at Wakefield, in Yorkshire, and on New Year's Eve 1460 she won a complete victory. The Duke of York was captured and beheaded, and such was the vengeance of the queen that she ordered the Duke's twelve-year-old son, the Duke of Rutland, to be executed as well. All the prisoners of rank, and there were many, were beheaded by the queen's orders.

The Duke of Somerset had been slain in battle at St Albans; the Duke of York was executed after the battle of Wakefield. Thus the dukes whose enmity had begun the Wars of the Roses were dead, but the war went on. Both Dukes had sons. The eldest of the Duke of York's three sons was Edward, Earl of March, and he, nineteen years old, vowed to avenge his father's death, and to overthrow the house of Lancaster. He was supported by many noblemen, chief among them the Earl of Warwick.

After her victory at Wakefield, Queen Margaret marched at the head of her army southward towards London. Previously in the war armies had caused as little disturbance as possible, for both sides wanted to enlist the sympathy and support of the country. Queen Margaret's army had no such scruples. It was partly Scottish and it was natural for the Scots to plunder and loot the 'foreign' towns and villages of England. Their northern English comrades followed suit; so every town and village through which Queen Margaret's army marched was plundered.

The Earl of Warwick was in London, the young Earl of March away in the west country raising troops. Warwick at once mustered another army and marched north to St Albans, to wait for the Queen. He had to guard two roads, so he strung his army out over a line four miles long, with his left flank in St Albans. While he had small detachments at vantage points all along the long line, his force was mainly divided into three columns, one in St Albans itself and the other two on the main roads from the north.

Warwick employed a number of new devices to hinder the queen's progress. He spread large cord nets in front of his position made with long sharp nails standing upright at the knots. He also had wooden lattices bristling with nails which were placed in gateways and gaps in hedges. Another new idea was called the caltrap. This was four sharp spikes so arranged that, however it lay on the ground, one spike stuck up, and they were scattered about the fields. It was like a modern minefield. But the most novel feature of Warwick's defences was a cannon fired with gunpowder and 'hand guns'.

The queen was between Luton and Harpenden, marching

straight towards the Earl of Warwick's position, when she received a message from a Kentish squire in the Yorkist army. It gave detailed information of the earl's position, and described the new devices prepared for her. Queen Margaret made a new plan, to bear right-handed through Dunstable and attack St Albans from the west. This brilliant strategy was most unusual for those days of frontal attack. If the queen could effect a surprise she would have to deal with only a third of the Yorkist force, and could proceed to attack eastwards along his line. All Warwick's clever 'minefields' would be wasted.

The plan worked. The queen's army marched southwards as expected, and then suddenly swung right-handed and fell unexpectedly on Dunstable in the evening of the 16th February, 1461, slaying or capturing the garrison of two hundred Yorkists. Without any delay the army set off on a twelve-mile night march to St Albans.

The advance guard reached the outskirts of the city as dawn was breaking. Surprise was complete, and there were no sentries and no barriers. It was not until they were in the heart of the town near the abbey that they met any opposition. The opposition they did meet, however, was highly effective. A party of Yorkist archers were on duty at this point and the deadly flights of arrows whistling down the narrow street drove the queen's vanguard back. The advantage of surprise was lost, and the abbey bells raised the clamour of alarm. Every Yorkist in St Albans seized his arms and hurried into the streets to take up hastily improvised defensive positions.

Meanwhile, as in the first battle of St Albans, another way into the city had been found. A column of the queen's advance guard, baulked down one street, got into the next and burst out into St Peters Street in the middle of the Yorkist defences. For the second time in six years the streets of St Albans were filled with fighting men, and the shouts and din of battle. This time the situation was reversed. This time the Lancastrians were fighting into the city. The Lancastrians heavily outnumbered the Yorkist garrison; as more and more of the queen's troops poured exultantly in the Yorkists were overwhelmed. Some escaped, most were ruthlessly slain.

While St Albans was being captured, the Earl of Warwick was busy with the complicated task of completely changing the direction of his line. From facing north it had to be turned to face St Albans in a south-westerly direction. By the time the queen had consolidated the capture of St Albans half of Warwick's line was in its new position. The queen's army, their morale high from their success in St Albans, hurried out of the city and drew up facing the enemy in the fields south of the town. The queen's force advanced, into a tempest of arrows, and engaged. The queen had a great advantage in numbers, but her men had marched throughout the night and had already fought hard. When their first surging assault on Warwick's line was furiously repulsed they fell back.

A second attack was launched, this time with better results. The lines swayed in close combat, but the Yorkists still stood firm. They knew that the remainder of Warwick's army, the right flank of the original line, was marching fast to join them. All they had to do was to hold out against the stronger enemy until the reinforcements came. The fighting was sustained for a long time, the lines locked together. Gradually, however, the greater numbers of the queen's army began to force the Yorkists back. Soon the strain became too much; the Yorkists' resistance suddenly snapped and they fled.

Thus it was that when the fresh Yorkist column, marching hard, approached St Albans they saw their comrades coming towards them in full flight. Panic is infectious and, as the defeated Yorkists stumbled towards the new column, that too halted, hesitated, and joined his comrades in retreat. Queen Margaret's victory was complete.

King Henry VI had spent the day of battle in the fields to the south-east of the city, sitting as before under a tree. When the defeat of his captors was sure, his guards fled, fearing the queen's vengeance if they were captured. The king asked the two French knights guarding him to stay, to protect him from any wild soldiers who might come his way.

Henry VI knights the Prince of Wales, St Albans, 1461

He was found by one of the queen's knights, and escorted with

divers lords to attend him to the Lord Clifford's tent, where the queen
and the young prince met him to their great joy. At the queen's request
the king honoured with knighthood thirty gentlemen who that day
had fought. The prince also was by him dubbed knight. Then they
went into the abbey, where they were received with joyous anthems.

Thus Edward, Prince of Wales, was knighted on the field of
battle at the age of seven. He was, however, something of a cam-
paigner, having narrowly escaped from the battle of Northampton, suffered a whole chapter of adventures with his mother, and
marched with his mother's army from Scotland, witnessing battles
at Wakefield and St Albans. It was a strange upbringing for a boy,
even if he was the grandson of Henry V. It certainly taught him
how to be harsh. When the two French knights who had guarded
the king, and had stayed at his request when all others fled, were
brought before the king, he turned to the prince. 'Fair son,' he
said, 'shall these knights die whom you see here?' It is said that the
little prince replied promptly, 'Their heads should be cut off.'
Both were immediately executed, with all others of rank who had
been captured.

The queen's brave ambition was realised. The red rose of
Lancaster was triumphant, the white rose of York was trampled
underfoot. The Earl of Warwick had fled, his army broken. The
king was free, to reign as she advised him, and no longer the cat's-
paw of the house of York. The inheritance of the Prince of Wales
had been saved. So thought Queen Margaret in her triumph at
St Albans.

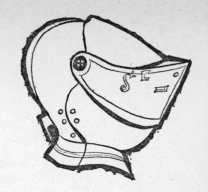

Chapter 6

The White Rose Triumphant

The Battle of Towton

29th March 1461

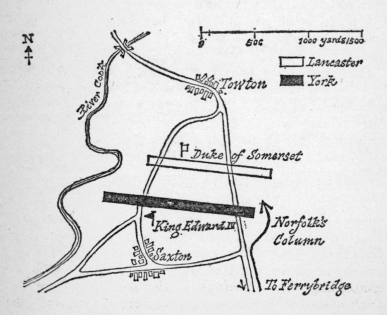

King Henry VI did not at once march to London after Queen Margaret's victory at St Albans. He waited in the hope that terms could be made by which he could enter London peacefully. This was a tragic mistake. If he had marched to London at once it is probable that the bells would have rung to welcome him, not so much for love of the house of Lancaster, but in relief at the end of the six years of war.

While the king delayed in St Albans his enemies were active. The head of the house of York, after the Duke was executed at Wakefield, was the young Earl of March. He had proved his prowess two weeks before the battle of St Albans by defeating a Lancastrian army at Mortimer's Cross, near Leominster in Hereford. The news of Queen Margaret's victory at St Albans spurred him to prompt action, and while the king and queen delayed their entry into London Edward marched there swiftly. So it was for Edward, Earl of March, head of the house of York, that the bells of London rang on the 26th February, 1461.

The Duke of York had been content to be King Henry's first minister, to rule the country ostensibly through the Lancaster king, and to have the promise of the succession to the crown after King Henry's death. His son was not so patient. Six days after entering London, on the 4th March, he had found himself proclaimed king – King Edward IV. London accepted him, and the southern counties. There were now two kings in England, the mild and vague Henry VI of Lancaster, who had been king from his earliest infancy, and the energetic and determined Edward IV of York, aged nineteen.

When he received the startling news that London had accepted the young Earl of March as king, Henry VI hastily withdrew to York. The strongly walled city was a safe base for the king and queen, and most of their friends were in the north. The fact that York became the headquarters of the house of Lancaster is one of the many confusing features of the Wars of the Roses.

Edward knew he would have to fight for his crown, and he set about raising a larger army than ever before. All the power of York was swiftly summoned. The speed with which the new king acted was in striking contrast to the muddle-headed procrastination of King Henry. Three days after his proclamation, King Edward sent the Earl of Warwick into the Midlands and the west to bring every Yorkist to his banner. Two days later, Lord Fauconbridge marched for the north at the head of a strong column from Kent. Two days after that, on the 11th March, Edward IV himself set off from London at the head of yet another very strong division. Warwick and Fauconbridge were ordered to meet him at Pontefract, twenty-five miles south of York.

Queen Margaret, for it was she and not King Henry who provided the driving force for the Lancaster cause, was well aware that the climax of their fortunes was at hand. It was no longer war between the king and rebels, but, in the eyes of half England at least, between two kings of England. She took measures as vigorous as the Yorkists to rally the full strength of Lancaster.

While the Yorkist columns were marching north an enormous Lancastrian army of something like forty thousand men was mustered and took up a position ten miles south-west of York, between the villages of Towton and Saxton, astride the road from the south. The army was commanded by the twenty-four-year-old Duke of Somerset, the son of the enemy of old York, whose quarrel had begun the Wars of the Roses, and who was killed in action at the first battle of St Albans.

Thus the Yorkists were commanded by the nineteen-year-old

King Edward, and the Lancastrians by the twenty-four-year-old Duke of Somerset. In 1461 many of the commanders in the field were young men, because so many fathers had been killed or executed in the previous six years. While the armies prepared for battle King Henry, the Queen and the Prince of Wales remained within the safety of the walls of York.

On Saturday, the 28th March, 1461, King Edward's advance guard, probing forward, met the Lancaster advance guard at Ferry Bridge, at the crossing of the River Ayr. The Lancaster troops had the advantage of the skirmish, but a Yorkist force crossed the river four miles upstream, forced their enemy to retreat, and chased them back towards Towton.

The river crossing secured, the Yorkist army advanced across the river and took up a position facing the line of the enemy. Each army occupied a slight ridge with the River Cook, then in spate, forming the western boundary of the battlefield. It was gently undulating open country, with patches of woodland to the west. Never before had two such mighty hosts faced each other in England as the seventy-six thousand who spent the night waiting for the day of battle.

Palm Sunday, the 29th March, 1461, dawned dully. The sky was overcast, with a threat of snow in the air, and a strong south wind blew in the faces of the Lancastrians. No move was made for four hours. The Duke of Somerset waited for King Edward to attack, and King Edward delayed because a column under the Duke of Norfolk had not arrived. It began to snow.

The first move was made by the Yorkists. Taking advantage of the fact that the snow, falling towards the Lancaster line, reduced their visibility to a few yards, Lord Fauconbridge ordered his bowmen to advance quietly to within range of the enemy and to fire *only one* arrow each. They were then to fall back quickly to the main line, out of range of the Lancastrian bowmen.

The ruse was successful. The Yorkist arrows flew into the Lancastrian bowmen, posted in the front line. They replied immediately, shooting blind into the snow. Although they could not see their enemy, they imagined from the arrows they had

The Earl of March proclaimed King Edward IV, 1461

received that he must be within range. But the Lancastrian arrows fell harmlessly into the ground where the Yorkists had been. When the Lancastrians had used all their arrows, Fauconbridge sent his bowmen forward to collect them.

This was but the overture to the battle of Towton. The battle proper opened when the whole Lancaster line advanced from their ridge and up towards the Yorkist line. As they came on, the Lancastrians were hotly received by the Yorkist bowmen, now well supplied with arrows. Men fell, but the gaps were filled from the rear and the long line of Lancaster climbed to the ridge and battle was joined.

The fighting, more furious than ever before in this civil war, lasted throughout the afternoon and into the evening. Never had there been anything like it. Both King Edward and Somerset had issued orders that no quarter was to be given. Every man knew that if his side lost the battle his life would be forfeit afterwards. All the anger, bitterness and vengeance accrued in the six previous battles found their vent at Towton. A great wall of dead and dying grew between the two armies.

The fighting was not incessant. There were intervals when each side paused to take breath, when exhausted men fell back and fresh men took their places. Very few details of this murderous battle have come down to us; perhaps those who survived wished to forget the madness and the horror of that Palm Sunday afternoon. One incident is famous, however. During one pause, Lord Dacres, commanding one wing of the Lancastrian army, went behind the line, sat down and took off his helmet to drink water. As he drank, an arrow pierced his throat and killed him. The arrow is said to have been shot by a boy whose father had been killed by Dacres.

As the evening closed down on that dreadful scene, Lancaster began to gain the advantage. For a moment it seemed that King Henry and Queen Margaret, waiting anxiously in York, were to win back the throne, and that young Edward of York's audacious assumption of the crown would come to naught. One circumstance, however, changed everything. The Duke of Norfolk's column arrived. It marched up the road from Ferry Bridge to the battlefield and deployed suddenly and violently against the Lancastrians' left flank.

The new attack turned the tide. All on that field were desperately weary and sick with the slaughter. Norfolk's attack was decisive. It drove back the Lancastrian left and soon the whole line was in flight, hurrying northwards up the road to Tadcaster. The River Cook was in spate and only the road bridge and two fords could be used. The Yorkists were in hot pursuit, and the slaughter at the fords was terrible. They said that soon fugitives and pursuers were crossing the river on bridges of dead bodies.

At last merciful night fell, and the killing stopped. The casualties at Towton were pitiful. There are no accurate records, and estimates vary wildly, but it is evident that the Lancastrian army lost something like twenty thousand men killed, York twelve thousand. Another twenty thousand Lancastrians were wounded or captured.

The battle of Towton made King Edward IV and the house of York supreme. Henry VI, his queen and his son fled to Scotland that night. The queen and the Prince of Wales took boat to France. Queen Margaret was not running away. She went to get immediate help from the king of France to continue the fight.

King Henry's fortunes were at low ebb. After a lifetime in palaces, treated by all with reverence, even when the Duke of York was in reality his master, he now lived for twelve months disguised as a peasant, a homeless vagrant lurking in the wild country of the border between England and Scotland. Eventually he was captured and taken to London. His feet were tied by leather thongs to the stirrups of a poor nag, and a straw hat was put on his head. In the presence of a large mocking crowd he was led three times round the pillory and then into the Tower. The gates clanged behind him, and he was thrown into a dungeon.

Henry VI was a miserable captive in the Tower for seven years, and then suddenly the wheel of fortune turned. The Earl of Warwick quarrelled with King Edward. The peace after Towton had been an uneasy one. Englishmen had too many old scores to settle, fathers, brothers and sons killed, and insurrections were always breaking out. Taking advantage of these, Warwick entered London, proclaimed poor King Henry again and led him from the Tower to the palace. So complete was the change in fortune that Edward IV had to fly to France. But six months later he came back. At the ferocious battle of Barnet in April, 1471, the Earl of Warwick was killed. Edward IV returned to London as king, and Henry VI was taken back to his dungeon, never to leave it alive.

Queen Margaret never gave up hope, never relaxed in her unceasing efforts to win back the throne for her husband and the succession for her son. The year after the battle of Towton she landed in Northumberland with a French army, but the venture failed, and she returned to France. Ten years later, early in 1471, she landed at Weymouth, rallied strong support for the red rose, and marched to Bristol, her force growing as she went. The Prince of Wales, now eighteen, commanded the centre division.

From Bristol, Queen Margaret marched north and at Tewkesbury she turned to face the army King Edward led to meet her. At the battle of Tewkesbury, in May, 1471, even the indomitable Queen Margaret was utterly and finally overthrown. King Edward was completely victorious. The Prince of Wales, fighting bravely, was taken prisoner and within a few hours he was stabbed to death, perhaps by the hand of, certainly in the presence of, King Edward's brother, Richard, Duke of Gloucester. Queen Margaret was captured in a near-by convent. She was cruelly mocked and thrown into prison. After five years in prison she was escorted to France and lived for a further six years in loneliness and poverty. Immediately after the battle of Tewkesbury, Richard of Gloucester rode fast to London bearing a warrant from his brother the king. He hastened to the Tower and the long miserable life of Henry VI was ended with a dagger.

The white rose of York was triumphant, the red rose of Lancaster was thrown down. Henry VI was dead, the Prince of Wales was dead, Queen Margaret could plot no more. As King

Edward VI rode back to London he could have said, as Shakespeare makes him say at the end of *Henry VI, Part 3* –

> *Once more we sit in England's royal throne,*
> *Repurchas'd with the blood of enemies.*
> *What valiant foemen like to autumn's corn*
> *Have we mowed down, in tops of all their pride!*

Chapter 7

The Marriage of the Red Rose and the White

The Battle of Bosworth

22nd August 1485

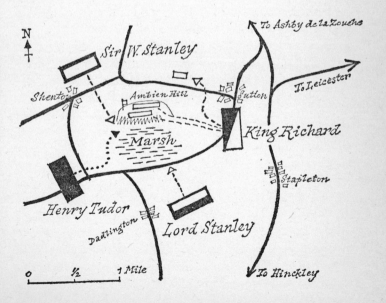

Edward IV reigned for twenty-two years, twelve of them after the murder of King Henry VI in 1471. He had but little comfort riding the restless and mettlesome steed which was England. The House of York was triumphant. But the spirit of Lancaster was not altogether broken, though all its leaders were destroyed and Queen Margaret was no longer free to maintain the relentless struggle. There were many in England who suffered the rule of York with an ill grace, and who thirsted for revenge on fathers, brothers and sons slain in battle or executed in the long civil war. It was, then, an uneasy realm that King Edward ruled.

The King died in 1483, aged forty-two, leaving two young sons and a daughter. These were Edward, Prince of Wales, aged twelve, James, Duke of York, aged ten, and the Princess Elizabeth of York, aged eighteen (see the family tree on pages 60–61). The Prince of Wales was proclaimed King Edward V, brought from Ludlow Castle and entered London in state. He was lodged in the Tower of London, which was a royal palace as well as a State prison, and his coronation was arranged. The little Duke of York joined his brother in the Tower. The Duke of Gloucester became the King's Protector, an obvious choice as he was the boy's uncle and nearest relative of the blood royal.

In the family tree on pages 60–61 it will be seen that Richard of Gloucester had an elder brother, George, Duke of Clarence. But Clarence had been murdered in 1478. In the second campaign of the Wars of the Roses Clarence had fought for Lancaster. He was pardoned, but later tried for treason and murdered, it is said, by being drowned in a large barrel of wine. There is no evidence that Richard of Gloucester was involved in the murder of his brother, but it was said at the time that he did nothing to save him, and his death moved Gloucester one step nearer to the throne.

Richard of Gloucester was, then, Protector to the boy King Edward, and another look at the family tree will show that now only the two princes and the princess stood between him and the throne. Now came the first of two horrible and highly suspicious events. Richard called a parliament, a specially selected one, which declared that King Edward IV had been married before he married his queen, and so the three children were not true-born, and Prince Edward could not become king. The crown was formally offered to the next in succession, Richard of Gloucester, who pretended to accept it unwillingly.

Richard of Gloucester was proclaimed King Richard III, and he was crowned at Westminster in July, 1483. The coronation procession from the Tower to the Abbey, and the ceremony itself, were unusually magnificent; it was as if Richard wanted to make sure of his accession by much splendour. In the procession he was accompanied by three dukes (not many dukes had survived the wars), nine earls, twenty-two viscounts and barons and eighty knights. Richard himself was dressed gorgeously and rode a great white horse which, they said, looked as proud as Richard himself. Neither the royal princes nor the princess Elizabeth were there; the two boys were left in the Tower, the princess was in sanctuary, safely kept from her Uncle's power in a religious house.

Shakespeare makes Richard III a monster, with a hunchback, a withered arm and teeth like a dog. But Shakespeare drew the material for his plays from chroniclers living under Richard's enemy and victor, and it was natural for them to blacken Richard as much as possible. From people who wrote while Richard was alive we hear of no deformities of body. On the contrary, he seems to have been every inch a prince; handsome, well made and vigorous. He was also extremely ambitious, and, as events showed, capable of the deepest villainy to achieve his own ends.

The coronation was followed by a wonderful feast, and a few days later the new king set out on a royal progress through the Midlands, accompanied by his glittering court and a large number of fully armed men, well disciplined and splendid to see. Bells rang, people turned out and stared, some cheered. The fact was that although Richard had been popular as his brother's Lieutenant-General of the north and was admired as a great prince, the people of England were uneasy about the way in which he had become king. The sudden, and very convenient, displacement of the two princes and the princess looked very much like a very cruel form of cheating.

Richard realised that he would not be secure on his throne while the deposed Prince Edward and his brother lived. England had an affection for the merry and intelligent little prince, and was angry that he had been passed over. The second unforgivable event occurred. In August 1483, the two princes were murdered in the Tower.

People have tried to prove that Richard was not guilty of this terrible crime. They say that the princes were murdered by Richard's successor, Henry VII, and whole books have been written to try to prove this. Yet the facts point to Richard's guilt. In 1484, while Richard was still king, there was an outcry for the princes to be produced. It was announced that they had died. If the princes had died naturally, which would have been strangely convenient for Richard, their bodies could have been seen by doctors and they could have been buried according to their high rank. But the princes had disappeared. In 1675, nearly two centuries later, some workmen, removing a flight of stairs in the Tower, discovered some small human bones. They were examined and found to be the remains of two boys aged about twelve and ten. This evidence matched the confession, made afterwards, of two of the murderers, Tyrrel and Dighton, which confession the supporters of Richard claim to have been obtained by torture and therefore to be valueless. Yet they described burying the murdered princes under the stairs, and the discovery of the bones proves that part of the confession to have been true.

Another piece of evidence against Richard is that the news that the two princes had been murdered was announced to the French government in 1484, a year before Henry Tudor became king. That clears Henry of blame, and with Henry cleared, Richard becomes guilty. Richard had arranged for the princes to be declared baseborn, and so had become king over their heads. He was the only person to benefit from their death. It is reasonable, therefore, to add this most horrid double murder to the previous murders in which Richard was involved, and it is a long list: Edward Prince of Wales after Tewkesbury, King Henry VI, the boy King Edward V's uncles on his mother's side, and lastly, the princes in the Tower.

There was deep dismay in England, which took the form of an insurrection. Richard put it down, and executed the leader, his one-time friend the Duke of Buckingham. England was accustomed to executions and murders in the stormy and bitter contest between Lancaster and York. That seemed to be over, with York supreme in King Richard. But this callous murder of the two boys in the Tower horrified England.

A rhyme which was nailed to the door of St Paul's Cathedral was quoted everywhere. It was:

> *The cat, the rat and Lovel our dog*
> *Rule all England, under a hog.*

The first line referred to William Catesby, Richard Ratcliffe and Lord Lovel, Richard's three chief ministers. The 'hog' was Richard himself, whose badge was a boar. The king was aware of his unpopularity and tried to make amends by good legislation; but legal reform was not enough to win pardon for his crimes.

The nation-wide discontent was ideal for all those, and they were many, who still cherished loyalty to the House of Lancaster, for the red rose was not forgotten. It was only thirteen years since the battle of Tewkesbury, and memories were long. Henry VI and his son had been murdered, Queen Margaret had been thrown into prison, the Lancastrian leaders had been slain or had fled. But the old hatreds endured and new leaders were watching and waiting. One Lancastrian leader in particular was watching England from exile in Brittany; Henry Tudor, Earl of Richmond.

Henry Tudor was twenty-seven years old in 1484 when King Richard's young son died. As King Richard had no heir, Henry Tudor became next in succession, for he had royal blood. From the family tree on pages 60–61, you will see that his father, Edmund Tudor, had married Margaret Beaufort, great-grand-daughter of John of Gaunt by his second marriage. Thus he was descended from John of Gaunt, as were Henry IV, Henry V and Henry VI, and he was of true Lancaster blood. Henry Tudor's grandfather, Owen Tudor, had married Queen Katharine, the widow of Henry V and daughter of the King of France, which gave Henry Tudor French royal blood as well. A further claim was made for him, though a somewhat shadowy one, to be descended from the great Cadwallader, the partly mythical king of ancient Britain, who died in the year 684.

Henry Tudor thus had royal blood; and he was also a leader born. He was attractive, intelligent and clever, and the Lancastrian exiles in Brittany turned to him to champion their cause. His character had been forged in adversity. During his boyhood he had been besieged in Harlech Castle for seven years, and after the battle of Tewkesbury had to flee the country, when he was fourteen, into exile.

The exiles about Henry Tudor in Brittany grew as one man of rank after another slipped away from King Richard's unhappy court; unhappy because it was fraught with suspicion and uneasiness. Plans were made, and in the summer of 1485 a fleet was collected at Harfleur. On August 1st Henry Tudor sailed, with two thousand men, the English exiles and a thousand or more French mercenaries, confident of increasing this small force to a substantial army in England and Wales.

The fleet put in to Milford Haven, in south-west Wales and Henry Tudor stepped ashore, kneeling to kiss the sand and recite a psalm. He had landed in south Wales knowing that his Welsh blood would rally support in the early days of his march. There is an amusing story about King Richard's principal officer in Wales. When he was appointed, King Richard asked that his son should be sent to Court, so that if the officer proved untrue the son should be killed, for Richard III was so surrounded by enemies that he trusted no one. The Welshman saved making his son a hostage by swearing a great oath, that no rebels should pass through Wales, 'save they should pass over my belly'. The meaning was, of course, that he would be true to death.

When Henry Tudor arrived this officer was in a quandary. He could not let the Earl of Richmond pass because of his oath. The matter was solved by his standing under a bridge whilst Henry Tudor and his army marched over it, thus 'passing over his belly'.

Henry's army grew as he marched through Wales and into England. At Shrewsbury he had five thousand men, and he expected a further five thousand from the powerful baron Lord Stanley and his brother, Sir William Stanley. But Lord Stanley was not free, for King Richard had his eldest son, Lord Strange, as hostage to ensure Lord Stanley's loyalty. An arrangement was made by which both Stanleys would appear to remain loyal to Richard, and march on their own, but that when the battle was engaged they would join in on Henry's side.

When Richard heard that Henry Tudor had landed he acted with vigour. He marched to Nottingham at the head of his two thousand regular and well-trained men, to be in a good central position. Commands were sent to every county to muster armed men, to concentrate at Leicester. Richard himself rode round the Midlands, magnificent in shining armour on a great white charger, his gold crown set on his helmet, his men-at-arms riding behind him, the royal standard borne at his side. Richard sent a number of messages to Lord Stanley and Sir William Stanley to join him, but they tactfully remained aloof, though giving the king the impression that they were loyal.

From Shrewsbury Henry Tudor marched boldly eastwards

towards Leicester, where his scouts had reported that the king's army was assembling. He marched through Newport, Stafford, Lichfield, Tamworth and Atherstone, and camped for the night of 21st August some three miles south-west of Market Bosworth. Henry had another secret meeting with the two Stanleys, but still they dared not commit themselves, but repeated their promise to be at hand ready to join Henry when the battle had begun.

King Richard was at Leicester when he learned that Henry Tudor was marching resolutely towards him. He marshalled his divisions at once and set out from Leicester on August 21st, marching west through Peckleton and Kirkby Mallory, making camp in the evening at Sutton Cheney, no more than three miles from the enemy camp. Scouts of both armies were out – they called them scurryers – and the king's scouts occupied and held Ambien Hill, a small ridge about six hundred yards long which would provide a good defensive position. The king gave orders to take up position on the hill at dawn.

The two Stanleys had been ordered to join the royal army, but they still held aloof, and camped apart from the other two armies. Their positions were interesting and were to affect the whole course of the battle fought on the following day. Lord Stanley camped between the villages of Stapleton and Dadlington, midway between the main armies and to the south. Sir William Stanley took up a similar position north of the main armies, also midway between them, near Shenton. Thus the four armies formed a square, with the two Stanleys occupying the north and south sides. It was as if they were on the touchlines of a football pitch three miles long, each at opposite ends of the halfway line.

At dawn on 22nd August, 1485, a most historic date, King Richard's leading division marched to Ambien Hill and took up its battle position, followed by the centre division. Neither of the Stanleys moved, and both could be seen from the hill, their armour and arms shining in the morning sun. King Richard sent a stern order to Lord Stanley to join him at once on the hill, saying that if he refused, his son, Lord Strange, would be instantly beheaded. Lord Stanley could no longer put the king off with vague promises. His reply was simple: 'Sire, I have other sons!'

When King Richard received that answer he at once ordered young Lord Strange to be brought forward and executed. The officers hesitated and then one of them looked to the south-west. Pointing, he said, 'Sire, the enemy is past the marsh. After the battle, let young Stanley die.' King Richard looked where his officer pointed, and saw that there was no time for anything but battle.

The lower slopes of the hill were marshy, and Henry Tudor's army was advancing, swinging left-handed to keep on dry ground. Formed into two divisions, it was led by the Earl of Oxford. Henry Tudor marched under his two standards, St George, and the Red Dragon of Cadwallader. King Richard watched the enemy approach, their ranks confused by the diversion caused by the marsh. As they marched up the rising ground towards his position on the ridge, Richard looked to right and to left, but neither Stanley had moved. Henry Tudor glanced towards his flanks, too, wondering if the Stanleys would indeed join him. Without them he was doomed to failure, advancing up hill on an enemy occupying the advantage of position, with five thousand against eight thousand. He could but trust the Stanleys, so he marched on towards the motionless royal army.

Richard had formed his three divisions in column. The van, commanded by the Duke of Norfolk, stood on the top of the ridge. The centre, commanded by the king himself, was behind in support. The rear division, under the Earl of Northumberland, was three-quarters of a mile behind, in reserve. Richard could have sent Norfolk's division down the hill to attack while Henry's two divisions were confused after their change of course, but he stood fast.

As soon as Henry's leading division came within range the bowmen of both armies let fly, and the air was thick with whistling arrows. Henry had some cannon, too, which he had brought from Shrewsbury, and these joined in the opening bombardment. Cannon balls were found long afterwards. The noise of cannon fire was the signal for the Stanleys to advance. They raised their banners, sounded trumpets and began to move towards the battlefield, from their positions two miles or more to the north and south. Henry Tudor and King Richard saw them; Henry expected and King Richard hoped they were coming to fight for him.

The duel of longbows ended with the expenditure of the arrows and the two armies advanced on each other and clashed in close combat. The Duke of Norfolk led King Richard of York's advance guard down the hill, the Earl of Oxford led Henry Tudor of Lancaster's advance guard up the hill, and once again battle was joined between the white rose and the red. The fighting was fierce and with advantage to neither side. Henry Tudor's second division came up, to be met with Richard's centre. Richard turned and signalled to the Duke of Northumberland to bring up the reserve. But Northumberland did not move. He was watching the approach of the two columns from the wings. If they threw their weight in the battle for Henry Tudor, he must win and Northumberland preferred to wait and see what was to happen.

The battle was in suspense for a short time. Sword and pike flashed in the August sun, war-cries, shouts and cries of agony filled the dust-laden air. King Richard III watched, and then, suddenly, he realised that he was doomed. The cavalry advancing under the Stanley banners had wheeled slightly and it was obvious that they were bearing down to fight for Henry Tudor. An anguished glance behind him showed that Northumberland was still playing the traitor, was still waiting.

There was one slight chance for Richard to save the day, a chance which would only be seen by a fighter of great courage. King Richard called for his charger, his squire helped him into the saddle. Clad in his costly armour, with the white surcoat emblazoned with the leopards of England and the fleurs-de-lis of France, his gold crown on his helmet, King Richard drew his sword. He called his bodyguard to him and the glittering and resplendent cavalcade rode down the hill. King Richard led them towards the centre of the battle-line, set his horse to the canter

King Henry VII crowned on the battlefield of Bosworth, 1485

and then to the gallop. His purpose, desperate in the extreme, was to fight his way through to the standards of St George and Cadwallader, to slay, with his own sword, his rival of the red rose. Either he would with one blow destroy his enemy, for with Henry Tudor dead the day would be his, or he would die a true Plantagenet king, fighting to the end.

Henry Tudor's guards drew close to him, knights formed up, stirrup to stirrup, and someone led Henry Tudor back. With his sword whirling and flashing, King Richard fought his way through the press of battle. He was unhorsed, but scrambling to his feet he strode on, warding off desperate blows, fighting madly and tremendously until at last he was struck down. His crown rolled away and a soldier hastily hid it under a thorn bush, to be collected later. Thus died, in a splendour of fighting, the last king of the House of York. The red rose was at last triumphant; King Henry VI, his son, Queen Margaret, and all those of Lancaster who had perished, were revenged.

King Richard's two-year reign ended with ignominy, for his body was stripped, stabbed and, slung over a poor nag, taken to Leicester. He had become the most hated king who ever ruled England, and a long list of cruel crimes is attached to his memory. But at Bosworth, on 22nd August, 1485, he died a true warrior's death.

Fighting ceased with the death of Richard. Men who had been fighting desperately threw down their weapons and embraced. A crowd gathered round Henry Tudor, cheering him. Someone found the crown under the bush, dented and dusty, and Lord Stanley placed it on Henry's head, and there was a great shout – 'Long Live King Henry!'

A new age was born at that moment, and a new England. The first Tudor king was crowned. King Henry VII of Lancaster married the Princess Elizabeth of York. The old wounds were healed, in the marriage of the red rose and the white.

Chapter 8

Lambert Simnel the Pretender

The Battle of Stoke Field

16th July 1487

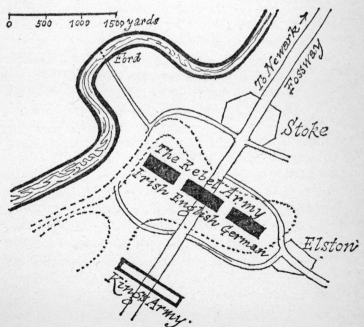

When Henry VII won the crown at the battle of Bosworth, England was in need of peace after thirty years of civil war. The new king was determined to give his country peace, with a strong central government. He took steps to keep the warlike and quarrelsome nobles firmly in their place.

The most dangerous nobles were banished or fled to France. The others were pardoned on promising good behaviour. To make sure, King Henry limited the number of armed retainers a nobleman could have, so that they had to disband their private armies.

Two persons had to be watched particularly carefully: the Earl of Warwick and the Earl of Lincoln; both had direct claims to the crown by birth. Edward Plantagenet, Earl of Warwick, was ten years old, the son of the Duke of Clarence who had been murdered in King Richard's reign by being drowned in a barrel of wine. The boy was the nephew of the two preceding kings, Edward IV and Richard III. Edward IV's two young sons, the 'Princes in the Tower', had both been murdered. Thus Edward of Warwick was the direct heir to the crown of Richard III.

Young Edward Plantagenet had not had much of a life, for his uncle, King Richard, had kept him in a dungeon in a distant castle. A contemporary chronicler wrote that this unhappy boy was 'kept out of all company of men and sight of beasts, so that he scarcely knew a hen from a goose'. Henry VII brought him to

London and put him in the Tower, locked up again, so as to be out of harm's way as a claimant to the throne.

The other person Henry had to watch was John de la Pole, Earl of Lincoln. He, too, was of the blood royal, as his mother was a sister of Edward IV and Richard III, and Richard had publicly named him his successor. King Henry VII was unusually merciful for those rough days. Most of his predecessors would have cut off Lincoln's head or had him discreetly murdered; but Henry let Lincoln live, after he had begged for mercy and sworn allegiance to the new king.

It was a costly error of mercy, for two years after the battle of Bosworth, Lincoln was marching on London at the head of a rebel army. Meeting him near Nottingham, Henry had to fight a long, hard battle at Stoke Field, where five thousand men were killed. Although the Earl of Lincoln commanded the rebel army, he was not claiming the throne for himself, but for a ten-year-old boy who rode beside him at the head of the army.

Everyone except Lincoln and a few close friends believed that this boy was Edward Plantagenet, Earl of Warwick, and now proclaimed and crowned King Edward VI. The truth was that the splendidly dressed boy who rode beside Lincoln was the son of an Oxford tradesman; he was not Edward Plantagenet, he was Lambert Simnel.

The story of Lambert Simnel is amazing. It is not clear whether his father was a shoemaker, a baker, a pastrycook or an organ-maker, but certainly he was only a humble Oxford tradesman. One day a priest named John Symonds noticed Lambert, and a series of events were set in course which led to the boy's coronation in Dublin as King Edward VI of England, France and Ireland. Contemporary accounts all agree that Lambert was a remarkably good-looking and intelligent boy. He was, wrote one, 'a childe of pregnant wit and comely personage'. He also looked exactly like the Earl of Warwick, and it was this fact that Symonds noticed.

Symonds must have been a most gifted teacher, for in less than a year he taught Lambert to speak and bear himself as a prince. He taught the boy the intricacies of court etiquette, the traditions and customs of a royal prince, and gave him the knowledge and confidence necessary for the extremely difficult part he had to play.

While Lambert was being trained to be a prince in some hidden place, much secret activity took place in the outside world. Lord Lincoln and a small number of ex-Yorkist leaders decided to use the Oxford boy to raise the country against Henry VII. Perhaps they genuinely believed that it was unjust that a Tudor and not a Plantagenet should be on the throne; more probably they saw an opportunity to win power for themselves.

Lincoln went to the Court of the Dowager Duchess of Burgundy in Flanders. This lady was a sister of King Edward IV and Richard III, and, naturally, she strongly resented the new Lancastrian king. The Duchess was powerful and wealthy. She provided money for the rebellion and hired two thousand German soldiers, professionals of the very first quality, commanded by General Swart.

Then Lincoln and his exiled Yorkist friends went to Dublin, where they were joined by General Swart and his two thousand German soldiers. The Earl of Kildare, who governed Ireland for Henry VII, and his brother, the Lord Chancellor of Ireland, joined the confederacy, and so did the Irish chieftains, following Kildare's lead.

Early in the year 1487 Lambert Simnel, known to everyone now as Edward Plantagenet, Earl of Warwick, was taken to Dublin and received as a royal prince. All but the few in the secret believed that he was really Edward Plantagenet. He was proclaimed King Edward VI, and crowned with all the traditional pomp and pageantry in Christ Church Cathedral, Dublin.

It is astonishing to think that a ten-year-old tradesman's son should have been able to act his part through the long and difficult ceremony of the coronation, in the presence of the nobility, the judges, the bishops, and the vast concourse of people. But he did not make a single mistake to betray the fraud. Wearing the heavy coronation robes, he was crowned and given the sceptre, orb and the spurs. He returned to Dublin Castle for a great banquet in a triumphant coronation procession.

When the boy 'king' was consecrated and crowned, the fleet was mustered and the army sailed to England. It landed on the Lancashire coast at the Pile of Fowdrey on the 4th June, 1487, and set off across the Pennines towards York.

When the news of the coronation in Dublin reached London, the king had the unfortunate Earl of Warwick taken from the Tower and paraded on horseback through the City of London so that everyone might see that the 'Earl of Warwick' who had been crowned king in Dublin was an impostor. Not everyone, however, was convinced. Many believed it more likely that the pale and pathetic boy shown to the Londoners was the impostor.

The king was at Kenilworth at the beginning of June when news was brought to him that the rebel army had landed in Lancashire. He acted quickly. Messengers were sent out ordering a rendezvous of the army at Nottingham. The king himself called up the local levies around Kenilworth and marched through Coventry, Leicester and Loughborough, increasing his force as he went. When the king marched into the camp near Nottingham he found six thousand men awaiting him, giving him a total strength of some ten thousand.

Before the rebel army reached York, news came to them that King Henry was marching north to meet them. Lincoln knew that the sooner the matter was decided by battle the better. The rebels had believed that as they marched across England men would hasten to join them. But very few joined the rebels and, indeed, some of the English who had come from Ireland began to melt away.

The Earl of Lincoln halted short of York and marched south to meet Henry, through Tadcaster to Castleford, down the old Roman Ryknield Street to Rotherham, and thence on to Southwell, five miles to the west of Newark. Here the army halted, for Lincoln's scouts had brought the news that King Henry was encamped at Nottingham, only twelve miles away.

Thus it was that on the evening of Friday, the 15th June, 1487, the two armies, King Henry's of ten thousand and Lincoln's of eight thousand, prepared for battle.

Soon after dawn on Saturday, the 16th June, messengers brought Lincoln the news that the royal army was breaking camp. Lincoln's plans had been made at a Council of War the night before, and trumpets and drums called the army of 'King Edward VI' to arms.

It was the custom for the commander-in-chief to ride along the ranks of his men before battle to encourage them by his presence. It is probable, therefore, that Lambert Simnel, the tradesman's son from Oxford, rode along the ranks of the rebel army on that June Saturday morning. What were the feelings of that ten-year-old boy?

He would be wearing armour, and these were the days when the armourer's craft was at its most skilful. His linen surcoat would be emblazoned with the Arms of England, the leopards and fleurs-de-lis, in red and blue and gold. Possibly a slender crown was fitted to his helm. Preceded by his standard bearer holding the royal standard, he would ride along the lines on a richly caparisoned pony. With him would ride the Earl of Lincoln and the other leaders, all in full armour shining in the morning sun, all with their squires and standard bearers, a jingling, glittering cavalcade.

The army was in three divisions or, as they were then called, wards. One ward was the Germans of General Swart, swords and pikes in perfect array, men with the confident expression of well-disciplined troops. The next would be the English knights with their bands of archers, men in leather jerkins protected at the shoulders with steel, each with their six-foot-long bows and their quivers of arrows. The third ward was the Irish, described by Holinshed as 'beggarly, naked and almost unarmed'. These scantily clad, long-haired Irishmen were fierce fighters, deadly with their short spears, but sadly undisciplined.

Lincoln formed his line of battle across the Fosseway, the road up which the king's army was marching. It was a good position on

Lambert Simnel before the Battle of Stoke Field, 1487

the crest of a ridge, which gave him the advantage of looking down on the approaching enemy. His right flank was protected by the River Trent, his left was about a quarter of a mile beyond the Fosseway. The line was about a mile long, held by some eight thousand men.

The 'Royal' inspection finished, the boy pretender was taken to a place of safety behind the line, and the army waited for its first glimpse of the enemy vanguard, advancing up the Fosseway.

The royal army had a march of twelve miles from its camp near Nottingham. The leading division, of about five thousand, commanded by the Earl of Oxford, halted when it came in sight of the rebel army lining the ridge across their road. Safely out of range of the enemy archers, Oxford deployed his column into line of battle.

While only the royal vanguard was up Lincoln had the advantage in numbers; his eight thousand faced the royalist five thousand. So he took the initiative and attacked before Oxford's complicated manœuvre of deployment was completed. The rebel army advanced down the slope, and the archers were ordered to fire. Clouds of glistening arrow shafts, fired with the traditional power and accuracy of English archers whose forebears had fought at Crécy and Agincourt, sent horses plunging and rearing and emptied many saddles. Lincoln's cavalry charged and the battle was joined.

Henry's main ward was rather surprisingly several miles in the rear and for a long time Oxford's division was without support. It was also fighting uphill.

Fierce hand-to-hand fighting lasted for nearly three hours. When one flank of the royal line wavered and began to break, the sight was too much for the Irish. With exultant cries they set off in pursuit, slaying everyone they overtook. This undisciplined advance did much to lose the battle, for when the royal main ward came up one-third of Lincoln's army was scattered and out of hand.

Those watching with the boy 'king' would have seen the fierce mêlée which had been forcing the royalists down the hill begin to steady. Then, slowly at first, the rebels began to be driven back, up the hill again. Without their two thousand Irish and with the Germans and English already battle-weary, the arrival of new troops turned the tide. More and more fresh men arrived from the main ward, and suddenly it was over.

The survivors of Lincoln's proud army became fugitives, running for their lives towards the River Trent and to the safety of the other bank. Few reached the river. There is a ravine, still called the Red Gutter, where they were caught and butchered in their hundreds. Of those who did reach the Trent, many were shot by royalist archers as they swam across; others, worn out by the long fighting, drowned before they reached the other side.

An old chronicler pays tribute to the officers of Lincoln's army. He writes:

> the rebel army was at last overthrown, four thousand slain and the rest put to flight, but not one of their captains fled, for the Earl of Lincoln, the Lord Lovel, Sir Thomas Broughton, Martin Swart, and the Lord Gerardine Fitzgerald, and a great number of others, were found dead in the very places where they had stood, fighting. Though they lost the battle yet they won the reputation of hardy and stout soldiers. Only the Lord Lovel, some report, that attempting to save himself by flight, in swimming over the River Trent, was drowned.

The battle of Stoke Field, fought to put the ten-year-old Oxford boy on the English throne, was won by Henry VII at a terrible cost. Four thousand of the rebels and three thousand of the royal army were slain in those three hours on the 16th June, 1487.

King Henry marched on to Lincoln, where many rebel prisoners were hanged. Lambert Simnel and Father Symonds, the priest who had begun it all, were both captured. In those days the Church was so powerful that even for high treason such as this a priest would not be executed. But the sentence passed on Father Symonds was, perhaps, more horrible than hanging. He was sentenced to spend the rest of his life in solitary confinement, chained up in a dungeon.

The fate of Lambert Simnel is one of those titbits of history that everyone knows; King Henry made him a scullion in the royal kitchens. Why did he do this? Was it to show his scorn for so humble a rival? Or was it a genuine act of mercy, recognition of the fact that this boy of ten was only the innocent victim of ruthless and ambitious men?

It is comforting to record that Lambert's strange story had a happy ending. He grew up to become the Royal Falconer to Henry VIII. When we remember Henry VIII's love of sport and cheerful and lively nature, Lambert must have had one of the most pleasant jobs in the land.

At the time no one knew what had happened to Lord Lovel. Some thought he was killed in the battle, others that he was drowned escaping. Two hundred and fifty years later the mystery was solved. Some time about the year 1720 they were putting a new chimney in Minster Lovel, the family home of the Lovels, when they discovered a secret room in the cellars. Sitting at a table was the skeleton of a man. On the table was a book, paper, ink and pens, and a very old-fashioned cap. It was the skeleton of the gay and splendid Lord Lovel who had fought at Stoke Field and escaped. He had made his way home and, to avoid capture and execution, he had hidden himself in this secret room. There, through circumstances we shall never know, he had starved to death.

The victory at Stoke Field made Henry VII secure. One can wonder what would have happened if Lincoln had won. Would the shoemaker's son have been crowned King Edward VI in Westminster Abbey? Or would he have 'disappeared' so that the real Edward Plantagenet could have been crowned? Or perhaps that boy might have 'disappeared' too, so that John de la Pole, Earl of Lincoln, would have been crowned as King John II. That seems the most likely. But Lord Lincoln lost the battle of Stoke, and the Tudor dynasty was secure; the dynasty that gave us King Henry VIII and Queen Elizabeth I.

Note: The full story of Lambert Simnel may be read in the author's book *The Boy They Made King*

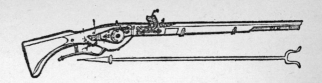

Chapter 9

King Charles and Parliament

The Battle of Edgehill

23rd October 1642

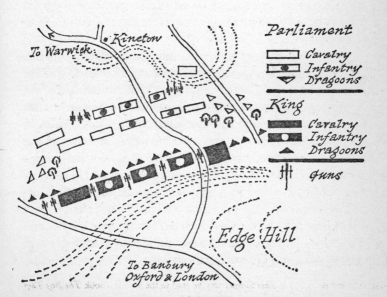

The battle of Edgehill was the first fought in England for a hundred and fifty years. Its cause has much in common with the battles of Lewes and Evesham four hundred years before; on one side was the king, on the other the king's government. In 1264 and 1265 the barons were demanding a regular Parliament; in 1642 Parliament was demanding more power. In the thirteenth century the quarrel was solved by two brisk battles, but in the seventeenth century the first battle proved to be the start of a long and bitter civil war.

How was it that two armies of Englishmen faced each other in arms at Edgehill on that October day in 1642? The battle was the climax of a long quarrel between king and Parliament. Until the death of Queen Elizabeth I, forty years before, the monarch, king or queen, was considered to rule absolutely, by 'divine right'. The sovereign could do no wrong and was, as it were, the owner of the country. He ruled personally, advised by ministers he himself chose. Parliament met when the sovereign summoned it and was expected obediently to act in accordance with the royal wish, usually to raise money.

Parliament was not always as meek as the monarch wished, and in the reigns of James I and Charles I it began to demand more power. To put the problem in its simplest terms, it was as if Parliament said, 'We are the elected representatives of the people. We should govern.' To this the king could have replied, 'I am the king. This land is mine. I alone know what is best for my people. Parliament may advise me, but I choose whether I take that advice or not.'

Parliament's challenge to the king's authority became increasingly severe. The parliaments of Charles I consisted of earnest and resolute men sincerely believing in the authority which Parliament should have. The majority of the members were Puritans, deeply religious and austere, their conduct and their beliefs based only on the Bible. The Puritans distrusted anything in the Protestant church which resembled the customs or beliefs of the Roman Catholic church. So relentless was their hatred of the Church of Rome that they wanted to dispense with bishops and many parts of the Protestant organisation and service. It was this Puritan majority in the House of Commons which provided the strongest opposition to the king, an opposition made more bitter by the fact that the queen was a Roman Catholic.

King Charles I was a sincere and upright man, a devoted husband and father. He genuinely believed that he alone knew how to ensure the peace and welfare of his people. He saw himself as the father of his subjects. Like the Puritans in Parliament, King Charles held to his beliefs to the point of obstinacy. The Puritan Members of Parliament were backed, of course, by great numbers of Englishmen who thought with them. On the other hand, there were a great many Englishmen whose instinctive loyalty was to the king and all he stood for.

Charles I came to the throne in 1625 and for the first fifteen years of his reign there were no dramatic results of the conflict between king and Parliament. But in 1640 a Parliament met, known afterwards as the Long Parliament, which brought matters to a head. It compelled the king to dismiss a number of his personal advisers and made him promise to call a parliament at least once in every three years, thus putting an end to the custom of the king's dismissing a parliament which did not act as he wished. The Parliament of 1640 made sure of itself by forcing the king to agree that it should continue in existence until it dissolved itself. Thus, without resorting to rebellion or arms, Parliament had wrested the main power of government.

In 1641 a rebellion broke out in Ireland. An army had to be raised to deal with it. Always in the past the king had controlled the army and he naturally expected to do so. The House of Commons, however, insisted on commanding the army. Their reason is obvious; with any army the king could dismiss Parliament and cancel their hard-won success.

King Charles had suffered his political defeats with admirable patience. This new challenge over the command of the army was more than he could accept. Events moved fast, and he decided, rashly, on bold action. One morning he went personally to Parliament at the head of a large armed guard and entered the Chamber to arrest the five Members of Parliament who were most active against him. Everyone in the House stood bare-headed, silent and angry. King Charles looked round the Chamber and saw that the five Members were not there. They had been warned a few minutes previously and had slipped away. Entering Parliament against the traditional privilege of the House brought matters to a head. The outcry against the king in London was so great that he left the capital and, his patience exhausted, determined to raise an army to put down by force this Parliament which was robbing him of all his royal authority.

On the 22nd August, 1642, King Charles raised his standard at Nottingham Castle, to summon all loyal subjects to fight to win back the ancient royal rights and privileges which Parliament denied him. The ceremony was rather sad. It was a wet, windy day; the herald who read the proclamation stumbled over last-minute alterations the king had made, and the wind blew over the royal standard.

Whatever the feelings of the people assembled at this symbolic ceremony, there were two who must have been considerably excited. These were the king's sons, Charles, Prince of Wales, aged twelve, and James, Duke of York, aged nine. Both were destined to reign, and nine years later Prince Charles was himself to march against Parliament with an army. It is fascinating to try to imagine the feelings of these two boys on that wet, windy day in August, 1642. Their father, driven by circumstances they could not understand, was declaring war against his own subjects. They would have been, like everyone else about the king, confident of speedy success. It is certain that they were very proud of their new and very beautiful suits of armour. They accompanied their father as he marched to the west country and back towards London, and they were both spectators at the battle of Edgehill.

The king's object was to march to London, and, with force where words had not prevailed, to dismiss this obstinate Parliament. From Nottingham he marched west to Shrewsbury to recruit from Wales and the west country. His commander-in-chief was the elderly Lord Lindsey, and his cavalry was commanded by his dashing and handsome young nephew, Prince Rupert of the Rhine, son of his sister Elizabeth, Queen of Bohemia.

There had not been a battle in England for a hundred and fifty years, since Flodden in 1513 when James IV of Scotland invaded England and was killed in action. The king's troops, therefore, were inexperienced, and inadequately equipped. The exception was Prince Rupert's cavalry. The prince, although only twenty-three, had seen active service on the Continent, and he quickly trained his men. They were naturally good horsemen and well mounted, and, to a man, they adored their high-spirited young commander.

The formal ceremony of raising the royal standard at Nottingham may have been marred by wind and rain, but the royal proclamation found a response in the hearts of many Englishmen. The king declared that if God gave him victory he would maintain the Protestant religion, support the just privileges and freedom of Parliament, and govern according to the laws of the land. The assurance about maintaining the Protestant religion was intended to soothe the fears of Puritans who had suspected the king of leanings towards the Church of Rome. The promise to support the just privileges and freedom of Parliament was directed at those who were jealous of the new power and authority of Parliament and who thought the king wished to rule without it.

There were many, however, who wondered what the king

really considered as the 'just privileges and freedom of Parliament'. But the royal proclamation appealed to a great number of moderate men who had been shocked by the stubbornness and extreme demands of the Puritan majority in the House of Commons, and these formed the greater part of those who rallied to the king.

The composition of the opposing sides in the conflict between the king and Parliament followed no set pattern. It was not the noble against the commoner, the rich against the poor; it was not north against south, nor east against west. Nor was it a war of religion. There were men of rank on both sides; gentlemen of ancient family supported Parliament, and many a yeoman and tradesman gave his savings, and even his life, for the king. Each army was a cross-section of the country.

There was, however, a marked difference, in a general way, between the two sides. The Royalists, or Cavaliers, tended to see the war as a romantic adventure; their approach was light-hearted and gay. They were ready to fight and die for their king, who represented the colourful traditions of the past. Those who supported Parliament, on the other hand, served as a solemn duty. They were equally ready to fight and die for their principles – government by Parliament – and for some of them, even more important, for a simpler Protestant religion. The traditional picture we have of the Cavalier in his wide-brimmed hat with a curly feather, and of the Roundhead soberly dressed and somewhat sour of expression gives a reasonable picture of the two sides in the war.

There were many families who took no part in the war, and the life of the ordinary people of the country went on undisturbed except, of course, when part of either army was in their neighbourhood. The story of Mr Shuckburgh shows the almost casual way in which men became involved. Shuckburgh was a Warwickshire squire, and one Saturday he was setting out from his country house with his hounds for a day's hunting when he was suddenly astonished to meet an army on the march. Wonderingly he watched it go past until he saw the king himself. Shuckburgh asked what it was all about. Someone explained, and Shuckburgh learnt for the first time that there was war between king and Parliament. He took his hounds back, gathered his tenants and rode off to join the king's army. He fought at the battle of Edgehill, with such distinction that he was knighted on the field.

While the king was raising and organising his army, Parliament was occupied in the same way. Parliament's main strength lay in London and the south-east. They had one great advantage in holding the ports, so that while no help could come to the king from his friends on the Continent, Parliament could move men and stores up and down the coast. The Parliament army, known as the 'Roundheads' from the round helmets, or 'pots', they wore, were commanded by the Earl of Essex, the son of Queen Elizabeth's favourite.

While the king was organising his army in the west, and preparing to march on London, Essex marched to Northampton. His orders from Parliament were, 'to rescue His Majesty's person and the persons of the Prince of Wales and the Duke of York, out of the hands of those desperate persons who were then about them.' No harm was intended to the king, and Parliament was careful to put the blame on his advisers.

When the king went from Nottingham to the west country Essex marched to Worcester, where he could prevent the king marching to London. It was at Worcester that the Royalists won their first success in a cavalry skirmish. Powick Bridge crosses the river Teme south-west of Worcester, and here Prince Rupert, with a body of cavalry, surprised some Parliament cavalry as they marched from a narrow lane. Rupert led his men in a furious charge which scattered the Roundheads so thoroughly that they galloped for nine miles with no one in pursuit before they pulled up. It was only a minor skirmish, but it was of great value to the spirits of the Royalists and a great embarrassment to the Roundheads. When the news of Rupert's success at Powick Bridge reached the Royalist army, everyone was convinced that a quick and easy victory over the Roundheads was certain.

The king's army was sufficiently complete and organised by the

12th October, 1642, and he was able to give the order to march
from Shrewsbury towards London. His intention was to take
Oxford as the base for his final march. His route was through
Bridgnorth, Wolverhampton and Birmingham to Kenilworth,
avoiding the Parliament strongholds of Coventry and Warwick.
It was only when the royal army reached Kenilworth on the 19th
October that the Earl of Essex at Worcester heard that the king
was on the march. He hastily set off in pursuit. It was a race
towards London with the king off to a good start. When the
Royalist supporters in London – and there were many – heard that
the king was on the road, they wore red ribbons in their coats and
jubilantly prepared a triumphant welcome.

The king was some thirty miles north of Oxford on the 22nd
October when he decided to give his march-weary men a day's
rest, using the opportunity to call on Banbury, the next town on
his route, to surrender and supply him with men and money. But
that evening a messenger brought the news that the Roundheads
were only nine miles behind him at the small town of Kineton.

This news made the king change his plans. If he continued
marching south with the enemy so close on his heels it would look
as though he were being chased, which would be harmful to his
dignity. Accordingly the decision was made to turn and give
battle.

The weary Royalist troops were summoned immediately from
their billets in villages around. The army marched back a few
miles to the top of Edgehill, a steep ridge three hundred feet high,
facing north-west. If you stand on Edgehill you see the country
stretching away to the north-west in a broad, flat plain. It was on
this ridge the Royalist army formed up at dawn on the 23rd October, 1642.

As the sun rose, the shine of armour and pike points along the
crest of Edgehill was seen by the Roundhead scouts. The Earl of
Essex sent messengers riding fast to call in his own troops from
the villages where they were billeted, and drums beat and
trumpets sounded as the Roundhead army prepared to march
forward towards Edgehill.

When day had fully broken the Royalist commanders realised that their position was not as wise as had first seemed; the crest of Edgehill was an excellent position for a defensive battle, but the hill was too steep for launching an attack. So the Royalist army advanced down the hill and formed up on the lower slopes.

While the Royalists were moving to their new position and manhandling their guns down the steep hill, the Earl of Essex took up his position in open country about a mile north of the king's army. Every man wore an orange sash for identification. Both armies formed up in the traditional manner of the time: the infantry in the centre, the cavalry on the wings, and the dragoons – mounted infantry armed with carbines – on the extreme flanks. The Royalists posted dragoons in front of their line as well. They were about equal in numbers, some thirteen thousand each, but the Roundheads had the advantage in guns and the Royalists were slightly stronger in cavalry.

In the century and a half since the last battle fought in England the archers had disappeared through the improvement in firearms. Half of the infantry were armed with muskets fired by a flint on the hammer striking against the steel above the touch-hole. The muskets were long and cumbersome, and a rest was used with a crook to hold the barrel. They fired a bullet weighing about an ounce and a quarter, with a range of four hundred yards, but they were only really effective up to two hundred yards. The other half of the infantry were the pikemen, armed with an eighteen-foot pike with sharp points. They could be deadly weapons, and with the butt rested against the right heel and held aslant they provided a bristling defence. The cavalry were armed with sword and pistol, and the dragoons with carbines, a shorter musket firing a lighter bullet. The infantry stood six deep, the musketeers in the centre, and the pikemen on the two flanks.

Throughout the morning, while both armies took up their battle positions, each watched the other warily. Neither was willing to strike the first blow. Many on both sides must have viewed the situation with dismay, wondering how the arguments and quarrels of the politicians had developed to the point when two armies of Englishmen faced each other in arms. It is as if they hoped for some miracle of good sense by which the quarrel between king and Parliament could have been resolved, so that the armed men could mingle and go to their scattered homes in peace. But there could be no miracle. Events had moved too far. By noon either army could have sounded the trumpets to attack, but no move was made.

One can imagine the feelings of the two young princes watching from a safe position on the slope of Edgehill, protected by a strong body of Life Guards. They could see their father's army, in the line of carefully placed formations, the banners of each regiment, and the royal standard, borne by Sir Edmund Verney, in the midst of a squadron of Life Guards. They could watch the colourful cavalcade accompanying their father as he rode along the lines. On their right they could see their jolly and admired uncle, Rupert of the Rhine, at the head of a thousand horsemen. It was a misty day, but they may well have seen the glint and colours of the enemy on the plain below them. A grandstand view of a set battle in open country is an experience granted to few boys.

The tense waiting of the two armies, which for a time seemed as though it would continue indefinitely, was ended by an incident which might be said to have started the great Civil War. A gunner in the Parliament army picked out the king standing with his staff on a little hill. Boldly attempting to make history, he aimed his cannon directly at the king. The slow-match was applied to the touchhole, and the cannon fired. The aim was good, but the range was short, and the ball fell in a field in front of the king – which is still called Bullet Field. Thus, the first shot was fired, and England was plunged into civil war which was to last, in one phase or another, for nine years.

This direct attack on his person roused the king to action and he ordered a general advance down the hill. At the same time the guns on both sides opened fire, the Parliament artillery doing the most damage because the king's guns, being on high ground, mostly overshot their target. The Royalist army had halted a few

Prince Rupert's charge at Edgehill, 1642

hundred yards before its enemy, and again both sides paused, still loth to begin.

It was Prince Rupert who took the initiative. He ordered his trumpeter to sound the charge, a charge which has stirred men's hearts ever since. If you have seen a horse at full gallop, you will know what a terrifying sight it must be if you were standing in its path: the horse with head raised, nostrils flared, thundering hooves charging swiftly towards you. Imagine, then, a thousand horses in the full charge, all excited by the trumpets and urged on by their skilled riders. There can be few spectacles more terrifying.

It was at the head of this thousand horsemen, born riders, confident of victory, riding for their king, that Prince Rupert of the Rhine charged the left wing of the Roundhead army. The long glittering lines of Cavaliers moved off, first at the walk, broke into the trot, into the canter, and finally charged at full gallop, reins loose, four thousand hooves pounding the earth.

The charge was so impetuous that the cavalry on the left flank of the Roundhead line broke and fled. A brigade of infantry next to them lost their nerve as well, and they, too, threw down their muskets and ran. It was a moment of triumph for Prince Rupert and his Cavaliers. They galloped after the scattered enemy, pursuing them right into Kineton and then up the road to Warwick. Some pulled up in Kineton to wreck the Parliament baggage wagons.

The Royalist cavalry on the left flank, commanded by Lord Wilmot, charged the right flank of the Roundhead line at the same time. It could not be as devastating a charge as Rupert's because the country was rough and broken by clumps of trees and crossed by hedges. Lord Wilmot missed the right wing of the Roundhead line and attacked the Roundhead reserve, breaking their formation with the fury of his charge and, like Prince Rupert, pursuing them towards Kineton.

With both flanks of the enemy broken, victory seemed certain for the king. He ordered his infantry to advance; colours were raised, and the drums beat loudly. The two lines of infantry engaged, fighting hand to hand, or, in the phrase of the day, 'at thrust of pike'. The young Duke of York, watching from the crest of Edgehill, later described it thus: 'Each line, as if by mutual consent, retired some few paces and then stuck down their colours (i.e. drove the flagstaffs into the ground) continuing to fire at one another even until night.'

The fighting of the two lines of infantry in the centre thus settled down to dour unflinching conflict. There were, however, two brigades of Parliament cavalry still intact on the right wing, commanded by Sir Philip Stapleton and Sir William Balfour, which had been missed by Lord Wilmot in his charge, and they now advanced. Balfour's brigade galloped through the Royalist left flank and attacked the king's guns. The gunners resisted, but were soon overcome. Then Balfour turned in his saddle and called, 'Nails! Nails!' They were needed to be driven into the touch-holes of the guns to render them useless – to spike the guns. But no one had any nails, so they cut the traces with their swords, so that the guns could not be moved, and rode back to the battle.

Another squadron of Parliament cavalry swept round behind the line and charged the Life Guards protecting the royal standard. The fighting here, as was natural for so important a prize, was furious. Gallant Sir Edmund Verney was killed, the royal standard was captured, and the Parliament cavalry rode away bearing it triumphantly aloft. Later it was recaptured by a Captain Smith, who was knighted in the field.

A third squadron advanced up Edgehill to where the Prince of Wales and Duke of York sat their horses amid their Life Guards. The officer commanding the Life Guards told the princes to ride back immediately, but Prince Charles begged to be allowed to stay. He drew his pistol, cocked it, and said, 'I fear them not, sir!' But the Life Guards hurried the princes back to safety.

When, at the beginning of the battle, the Royalist cavalry had swept their opponents away from the field, victory had seemed certain for the king. Now the tide of battle had turned. The very success of the Royalist cavalry proved to be an advantage for the Roundheads, for they had ridden away so fast and far in pursuit that the king had no cavalry when he needed them most. While the two lines of infantry fought stubbornly together, neither side giving an inch of ground, the Roundhead cavalry returned from their forays against the guns and the royal standard, and attacked the flanks of the Royalist foot. Thus the king found himself fighting desperately, not for victory, but to avoid defeat.

Dusk was falling when Prince Rupert and his Cavaliers rode back from their long pursuit. Horses and men were weary, too weary for further fighting. As the short October afternoon darkened, the fighting died down, as if by mutual consent. The two lines fell back to the positions from which they had begun the battle; each ignored the other. While the wounded were tended, soldiers sat close to their camp fires throughout the bitterly cold night, each army convinced that it had won the day. The Earl of Essex made a formal proclamation of his victory, and at dawn marched back to Warwick. Prince Rupert followed up harrying his rearguard, wrecking his baggage, and had the great satisfaction of blowing up his ammunition wagons.

The battle of Edgehill is usually considered to have been a draw. This does not seem quite fair. The king's intention was to march to London. The Earl of Essex intended to prevent him. Yet after the battle Essex withdrew northwards to Warwick, and the road to London was wide open to the king. There seems no doubt, therefore, that the Royalists won the battle of Edgehill.

The obvious course was for the royal army to turn about, form up and march immediately to London. This course was enthusiastically put forward at the council of war on the morning after Edgehill; but it was not followed. The king was by nature a man of peace. The slaughter and suffering of his subjects, inevitable in battle, grieved him. He did not want to take London at the cost of more lives. He believed that his subjects were equally horrified at the sight of Englishmen killing Englishmen, and he thought that the country would come to its senses so that no more fighting would be necessary.

Instead of marching directly to London the Royalist army advanced slowly through Banbury to Oxford, where the king was enthusiastically welcomed. Oxford was a good strategic position between London and the west, and a good base from which operations against London could be launched if they became necessary.

Meanwhile, the Earl of Essex made a wide detour to avoid the outpost of the royal army and returned to London, where Parliament considered what to do next. Letters passed between Parliament and the king, and a form of treaty was offered. But the terms were too harsh, and the king rejected them. At the same time, both armies were recruiting and reforming, and Roundhead detachments were posted outside the London area, covering all roads into the capital.

After two or three weeks at Oxford, the Royalist army set off cautiously towards London. It halted at Brentford, while the Earl of Essex took up a strong position at Turnham Green. The king had to decide whether or not to attack the Roundheads and try to fight through to London. Unwilling to plunge his subjects into another battle, he withdrew, first to Reading, where the Prince of Wales fell sick with the measles, and then back to Oxford. Here the king set up his court and settled down for the winter, hoping the whole conflict could be settled either by negotiation or by one final battle in the spring.

Chapter 10

Parliament Victorious

The Battle of Naseby
14th June 1645

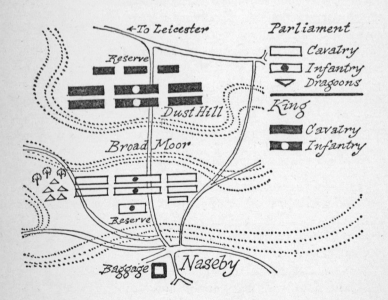

Both Royalists and Parliament had believed their quarrel would be ended by victory at the battle of Edgehill; and throughout the winter of 1642–3 both sides expected a settlement to be made. But the solution was not to be so easy, the difference between the two sides was too serious.

The king summed up his point of view seven years later. On the scaffold in 1649 he said, 'For the people I desire their liberty and freedom as much as anybody whomsoever; but I must tell you that this liberty and freedom consists in having government – those laws by which their lives and goods may be most their own. It is not their having a share in the government, that is nothing pertaining to them. A subject and a sovereign are clean different things.'

Englishmen who thought with Parliament could never agree that having a share in the government was 'nothing pertaining to them'. Most of them had a deep respect for the monarchy, but they could not believe that 'a subject and a sovereign are clean different things'.

So, because the points of view were so opposite, the Civil War continued. There were many minor actions and skirmishes, sieges of towns, castles and big houses. War is ugly and when men become soldiers they often behave with a brutality which would not be possible to them in ordinary life. When the Cavaliers captured a town there was looting, drunkenness and barbarism. The

Roundheads were by no means innocent of cruelty and plunder, even though they capped their victories with prayers and hymns. While the Cavaliers shocked people by their high-handed and high-spirited treatment of the conquered, the Roundheads gave offence by the wilful desecration of cathedrals and churches.

There was a strong and increasing Puritan influence in the Parliament army. The only religious authority the Puritans recognised was the Bible; any decoration in a church smacked of Popery. They stabled their horses in churches, smashed stained-glass windows, pulled down statues, and knocked the noses off effigies on tombs. We can see the result of this wanton destruction in many a cathedral and church today.

The conduct of the Royalists gave us a word – cavalier – meaning thoughtless and high-handed behaviour. The severe and humourless attitude of the Puritans, who considered dancing and the most innocent games as sin, was equally unnatural, and in the end it turned the people of England against them. The extremes to which some of the Puritans went are shown by the fantastic names they adopted, in all solemnity. There was, for example, a sergeant called Obadiah Bind-their-kings-in-chains-and-their-nobles-with-links-of-iron.

A number of major battles were fought in 1643 and 1644 as king and Parliament struggled for final victory. The most important battles in 1643 were Chalgrove Field, near Oxford; Atherton Moor, in Yorkshire; the capture of Bristol by Prince Rupert; and the battle of Newbury in Berkshire. In 1644 there were battles at Nantwich, Marston Moor in Yorkshire, and a second battle at Newbury. Some were Royalist victories, some Parliament victories, and some were indecisive. The most significant was Marston Moor on the 2nd July, 1644, in which Parliament won a great victory mainly through the military genius of Oliver Cromwell.

Oliver Cromwell, a country gentleman of Huntingdon, commanded a troop of cavalry at the battle of Edgehill with the rank of captain. Impressed by the success of the Royalist cavalry, he set about improving his own. He enlarged his troop into a regiment by recruiting proved men. He trained and drilled it hard and instilled into the men a discipline founded on religious zeal. His influence as a commander and his example in training troops spread through the Parliament army. His regiment, which soon grew into a brigade, fought with distinction in every major battle, so that in 1644 Cromwell was promoted Lieutenant-General.

Cromwell's cavalry, nicknamed the Ironsides, became an increasingly important part of the Parliament army, and at Marston Moor his brilliant generalship and the masterly fighting of his Ironsides brought an outstanding victory and paved the way for the final defeat of the Royalists the next year at the battle of Naseby.

As in the previous two years, the fighting quietened down in the winter of 1644-5. The king was in Oxford, where he had his court, his own rival parliament to that in London, and his headquarters. The Parliamentary army was completely reorganised as the 'New Model army', commanded by Lord Thomas Fairfax, with Lieutenant-General Cromwell, his second-in-command. The New Model army was a completely different proposition from the army which had faced the Royalists at Edgehill. It was well officered, well trained, and well equipped, and all ranks were inspired with a sincere and profound religious fervour. They were serious, solemn men, in strong contrast to the more romantic Cavaliers.

There were the usual skirmishes and minor actions in the spring of 1645. At the beginning of June Fairfax was besieging the city of Oxford with the New Model army while the Royalist army was forty miles to the north at Daventry, preparing to attack Fairfax. Rather than wait for the king to attack, Fairfax raised the siege and marched north, arriving at the village of Kislingbury, eight miles east of Daventry, on the 12th June.

The king was not ready for battle, so he broke camp and withdrew to Market Harborough. Fairfax followed and on the 13th June he was at Guilsborough, four miles south of Naseby. The Roundhead advance guard surprised a Cavalier patrol in Naseby as they were feasting and making merry at a long table in the courtyard of an inn. The revellers were all taken prisoner. The armies were now only eight miles apart, and the king decided that he must turn and give battle. The situation was the same as at Edgehill – if he continued his retreat northwards he would find himself being chased.

At dawn on the 14th June, 1645, the armies took up their battle positions. The Royalists occupied Dust Hill, a ridge about a mile south of the village of Sibbertoft. Fairfax occupied Red Hill Ridge, a mile north of Naseby. The armies were about half a mile apart, with a stretch of level land known as Broad Moor between them. Both armies were in the usual order of battle, infantry in the centre and the cavalry on the flanks. The king was in command, with Sir Jacob Astley commanding the infantry, Prince Rupert commanding the cavalry on the right, and Sir Marmaduke Langdale commanding the cavalry on the left flank. One brigade of infantry and two regiments of cavalry and the king's Life Guards were in reserve.

General Skippon commanded the Roundhead infantry, Lieutenant-General Ireton the cavalry on the left, and Lieutenant-General Oliver Cromwell the cavalry on the right. There was a reserve of two brigades of infantry, and on the left flank of the Parliament army the dragoons, dismounted to act as infantry, were posted among scrub land to protect Ireton's cavalry from the inevitable charge by Prince Rupert.

The king had in all seven thousand five hundred: four thousand cavalry and three thousand five hundred infantry. The Roundheads were greatly superior in numbers, almost two to one, with fourteen thousand: six thousand five hundred cavalry, one thousand dragoons, and six thousand five hundred infantry. Yet the Cavaliers were quite confident of victory. A Cavalier officer who said three weeks before the battle, 'Ere one month be over, we shall have a battle of all for all', felt sure that the king would at last be finally victorious. The Royalists called the New Model army the 'New Noodles', and believed the quality of their men would amply compensate for the odds against them.

The Roundheads were equally confident. Oliver Cromwell wrote afterwards of the battle:

When I saw the enemy draw up and march in gallant order towards us, and we a company of poor ignorant men ... I could not, riding alone about my business, but smile out to God in praise, in assurance of victory, because God would, by things that are not, bring to naught things that are. Of which I had great assurance, and God did it.

At ten-thirty in the morning, the royal army advanced from Dust Ridge. Every soldier wore a beanstalk in his hat, and as they stepped forward, cavalry and foot, in a long glittering line, they cheered and shouted the watchword of the day – Queen Mary! Fairfax ordered the advance too, and the Roundheads cheered and shouted their watchword – God our strength!

As at Edgehill, Prince Rupert of the Rhine began the operation with a tumultuous cavalry charge. He led his two thousand cavalry at full gallop straight at Ireton's cavalry on the Roundheads' left flank. Ireton's men succeeded in surviving the onslaught and tried bravely to hold the Cavaliers. But their impetuosity and fury were irresistible. Ireton was wounded in face and thigh, his horse was shot under him, and he was taken prisoner.

Thrusting aside all opposition, Rupert's horsemen smashed through their opponents, scattered them, and galloped on to attack the baggage in Naseby village, where a sharp engagement took place with the baggage guards. Prince Rupert did not stay long in Naseby; he remembered Edgehill, where his long pursuit of the flying enemy had deprived the king of his cavalry in time of need. He rallied his men and rode back to the battlefield.

Much had happened. The lines of Royalist and Roundhead infantry had met and were engaged in close and furious fighting. Despite their inferiority in numbers, the Royalist foot had from the first gained the advantage and were forcing the Roundheads back step by step. General Skippon was wounded and signs of panic began to show among the Roundheads. With Prince Rupert's success on the right and the increasing impetus of the infantry's advance in the centre, it began to look as if the day was to be the king's.

Two events changed everything. The Roundhead dragoons, who had been posted at some distance beyond the left flank of the line, had been untouched by Prince Rupert's charge. Seeing that their infantry was being forced back, the dragoons mounted and advanced briskly against the Royalist right wing. The dragoons were securely held off by the king's splendid regiments of foot. The flank attack by the dragoons did, however, bring some relief to the Roundhead infantry.

It was the second event which changed the whole course of the battle and, as it turned out, the course of English history. General Oliver Cromwell, commanding three thousand six hundred Ironsides on the Parliament right flank, had watched the progress of the battle, thoughtful and imperturbable. When Rupert charged on the king's right flank, Lord Langdale advanced with his cavalry on the king's left. The ground here was unsuitable for the gallop of a charge, being covered with furze bushes and full of rabbit holes. So Langdale's Cavaliers had to pick their way carefully over the rough ground. Their progress was watched by Cromwell, who at the right moment, when the Cavaliers were out of formation, ordered part of his own cavalry to charge them. Langdale's Cavaliers tried to form up, but before they could do so the Ironsides were among them and they were forced back and were soon in flight.

This happened while the Royalist foot were pressing the Roundheads back. Unlike Prince Rupert, Cromwell kept a close hold on his cavalry, checked them from pursuit, and brought them back. He then led his whole force against the left flank of the Royalist foot. It was a shattering onslaught, but the king's infantry, now thrown on the defensive, bore it magnificently.

The king, at the rear of the left with his staff, saw Cromwell launch his attack and realised that his only hope was an immediate counter-attack. He gave the order to advance and placed himself at the head of his Life Guards and led them towards the left flank of his line, where the fighting was the fiercest. One of his staff put his hand on the king's bridle and said, 'Sire, you will go upon your death?' Before the king could free his bridle, his horse had wheeled. Some commander imagined it was the king's intention to wheel away and gave the order, and the whole of the king's Life

Cromwell's 'Ironsides' at the Battle of Naseby, 1645

Guards and the reserve of horse behind them galloped away. They went half a mile before they could be stopped, and by that time it was too late.

This was the situation when Prince Rupert rode back to the battlefield. The Royalist infantry were making a gallant but hopeless stand, attacked in the front by the Roundhead infantry, on their right flank by the dragoons, and on the left flank by Cromwell's Ironsides. The king and the reserve had, through a mischance, temporarily left the field. Prince Rupert joined the king, and with his own cavalry and the king's Life Guards formed a new line to the rear of Dust Hill, to which the survivors of the Royalist infantry fell back.

Fairfax re-formed his line, and with Cromwell leading the cavalry on the right attacked the Royalists once more. But the king's soldiers had given of their utmost. The line held for a few moments only, and then broke. The victory of Parliament was complete. They took five thousand prisoners, including five hundred officers, all the guns and baggage, and all the king's correspondence. This was unfortunate because some of the letters from foreign governments were subsequently used against him. The king rode fast to Leicester, on to Ashby-de-la-Zouch, and back to Lichfield.

Attempts were made to gather a new army to take the field once more, but they were in vain. The battle of Naseby was the final victory. Events followed each other rapidly, a sad tale of surrender. Oxford and Bristol fell to Parliament, and one by one the Royalist strongholds were taken.

In May, 1646, King Charles surrendered to the Scots, who later handed him over to Parliament. The fate of the king was in suspense for two years. He escaped from captivity to the Isle of Wight, but he was recaptured and imprisoned more closely. Eventually he was taken to London to be tried for being 'a tyrant, traitor, murderer and public enemy to the Commonwealth of England'.

At his trial, spread over three days, the king was dignified and serene, firmly challenging the right of the court to try him. There were very few in England who wanted the king to be executed; there were, indeed, many among those who tried him who recoiled from the act; but it was considered to be necessary, and on the 27th January the king was sentenced to death.

As he was taken to Westminster Hall, many of the people who lined the streets wept, but he remained, as always, calm and dignified. He maintained his composure to the end. On the day before his execution his two youngest children were taken to see him – Princess Elizabeth, aged thirteen, and the ten-year-old Duke of Gloucester. The Princess wrote down what her father said:

> He wished me not to grieve or torment myself for him, for that would be a glorious death he should die, it being for the laws and liberties of this land, and for maintaining the true Protestant religion. He bid me read Bishop Andrew's sermons, Hooker's *Ecclesiastical Polity*, and Bishop Laud's book against Fisher, which would ground me against Popery. He told me he had forgiven all his enemies and hoped God would forgive them also, and commanded us and all the rest of my brothers and sisters to forgive them. He bid us tell my mother that his thoughts had never strayed from her and that his love should be the same to the last.

To the little Duke of Gloucester the king said,

> Sweetheart, now they will cut off thy father's head; mark, child, what I say: they will cut off my head and perhaps make thee king, but mark what I say. You must not be a king so long as your brothers Charles and James do live; for they will cut off your brothers' heads when they catch them, and cut off thy head too at the last, and therefore I charge you do not be made king by them.

The Duke of Gloucester stoutly replied: 'I will be torn to pieces first.'

Neither of the king's two eldest sons could see him, for they were both far away. The Prince of Wales had been made commander-in-chief of the king's armies in the west three months before the battle of Naseby and had gone with a Court and

Council of State, first to Bristol and then to Barnstaple. After Naseby he had withdrawn into Devon and Cornwall, then to the Scilly Isles, to the Channel Islands, and so to safety in France. Prince James, Duke of York, was in Oxford at the time of Naseby, and when the city was captured by Parliament he was taken away by them. Later he managed to escape and got away safely to Holland. Both Charles and James fought in England for the crown, as will be related in the stories of the battles of Worcester, Sedgemoor, and the Boyne.

The conflict between King Charles I and Parliament which had become war at Edgehill ended finally on the morning of the 30th January, 1649, when, on a scaffold outside the Banqueting Hall in Whitehall, the king was executed.

Chapter 11

Charles II Fights for His Crown

The Battle of Worcester

3rd June 1651

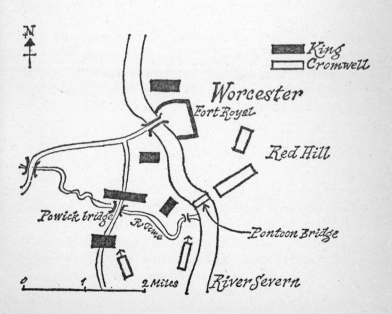

The twelve-year-old Prince of Wales who put on his new suit of armour at Nottingham Castle in 1642 was nineteen when his father was executed on the 30th January, 1649. When the monarch dies the heralds immediately proclaim his successor in the ancient formula 'The king is dead! Long live the king!' The proclamation was not made when Charles I died at the block, because the victorious Parliament decided that there should be no king in England. The country was to be ruled by Parliament and a Council of State, of which the dominant member was the Lord General, Oliver Cromwell.

In Scotland the tradition was not broken, and directly it was known that Charles I was dead the heralds proclaimed his eldest son King Charles II. The new king was a handsome dark man, more than six feet tall. He had a first-class intelligence, high spirits and wit. At the end of the Civil War he had escaped to France, whose king recognised him as the rightful king of England.

In France Charles lived in exile with his mother and his younger brothers and sisters. There was much travelling of messengers between the Scottish Government and the young exiled king in France. Highly secret plans were made, and Charles made many promises on religious matters, more indeed than he could have kept. The result was that in June, 1650, Charles landed in Scotland, to claim the crown of England by force of arms.

When Charles landed Oliver Cromwell was subduing rebellion

in Ireland. The Council of State ordered him to go to Scotland at once, and he took with him some of the regiments he had forged into highly trained and splendidly disciplined troops during the Civil War. Cromwell met a Scottish army on 3rd September at Dunbar, soundly defeated them and took up a position based on Edinburgh, ready to deal with Charles II or, as Parliament called him, 'the Pretender, Charles Stuart'.

The defeat at Dunbar was a serious setback to Scottish plans, but it by no means put an end to them. The army was reorganised and increased with recruits. Charles was crowned at Scone, the ancient place for Scottish coronations, on 1st January, 1651. Despite the presence of Cromwell's Roundhead army in the south-east of Scotland, plans went ahead for the invasion of England. On 6th August Charles led his Scottish army across the border near the west coast, at the head of twenty thousand men, of whom only five hundred were English.

It had been expected that the two armies would come to battle in Scotland, and there were long discussions in the Royalist council of war before it was decided to slip across the border round the west flank of Cromwell's army and march straight for London, hoping to outdistance the enemy. One factor which led to this decision was the expectation that many Englishmen would rally to the young king's standard. It was a reasonable belief, for half England had supported the Royalist cause in the Civil War. Many hearts would be stirred, it was thought, at the return of the young king marching to fight for his birthright.

The long colourful column must have presented a brave sight, the Scots in their plaids marching to the skirl of the pipes behind the royal standard. Charles set up his standard at Carlisle and was formally proclaimed king of England by his heralds. The ceremony was repeated in the market places of every town through which they marched. The route was Penrith, over Shap Fell to Kendal, and then on southwards through Lancaster, Preston, Wigan and Warrington. Here Charles intended to bear half left, to march through the Midlands to London.

But events did not turn out as Charles had hoped. In the

seventeenth century England and Scotland were virtually foreign countries. The English people bitterly resented the foreign invasion, the more so because the Scots looted towns as they marched through them. So Englishmen ignored the appeal of their late king's son when he came at the head of a wild and marauding foreign army who treated them like a conquered foe.

There was another unfortunate result of the looting. Many of the Highlanders, finding themselves rich with loot, deserted and made their own way back to the Highlands. Thus Charles got no recruits, and his army grew smaller as the Scots deserted.

When Cromwell heard that Charles had crossed the border he gathered his army and set off southwards for London by the eastern road. It became a race, with the length of England the course, London the finishing post, and the two armies as the contestants.

Cromwell's purpose was to march as fast as possible to fend the Royalist army off from London. Messengers were sent riding hell-for-leather ahead; two columns of cavalry, under Generals Harrison and Lambert, were despatched towards Wigan and Warrington to prevent the Royalists swinging leftwards towards London. The militia was called out throughout England to be ready to check the Royalists if they came their way, and to join the main column as it marched south.

In contrast to the cold and hostile reception accorded to Charles's Scottish army, the Roundheads were received joyfully at every town. The local militia were ready waiting to fall in, armed and equipped. Cromwell marched hard. It was a very hot August, and civilians marched beside the column carrying the soldiers' coats from town to town.

When the Royalists reached Warrington it was clear that the plan of bearing left for London would have to be changed, even though they still had the lead in the race with Cromwell's army. Their road through the Midlands was barred by the militia, and the squadrons of Parliament horse were harrying the flank of the column. So Charles continued southwards, towards the west country which had remained loyal to his father in the Civil War.

In the Severn valley he would be able to give his troops the rest they needed and, perhaps, at last, find a welcome and reinforcements.

From Warrington Charles led his Scottish army through Stafford, Wolverhampton and Kidderminster to Worcester, the 'Loyal City' of the Civil War, where he arrived on the 22nd August. There he decided to stand, to await the arrival of his enemy. The twenty thousand men who had marched across the Scottish border had dwindled to sixteen thousand.

Cromwell was thirty miles away at Warwick, with thirty thousand men. He marched through Stratford-upon-Avon to Evesham, where he was directly on the road from Worcester to London.

Cromwell made thorough and careful plans. He detached independent forces to block all the roads from Worcester, to cut off the enemy's retreat northwards, and to be able to catch any fugitives. With all his plans made, Cromwell marched to Worcester.

Worcester was then a walled and gated city. The River Severn, running north and south, served as a moat to the western walls, crossed only by the bridge at St John's Gate. The river was forty yards wide, with steep banks, and was a formidable obstacle. A mile to the south of the city the Severn is joined by the Teme, a swift-flowing river about ten yards wide.

The bridges across the Severn and the Teme were destroyed, except only the bridge from St John's Gate. Thus the two rivers provided natural defences for troops deployed in the meadows to the south-west of the town. Any attack from that direction, and it was the only practicable line of attack on the city, would have to be made across the Teme, and, if necessary, the defenders would be able to fall back and re-enter the city over the St John's Bridge.

An attack from the north or east would have to be made against the strong fortified walls. The only other possible point of attack was at the Sidbury Gate at the south-east of the city, and here Charles built a defensive position on a mound outside the gate, called Fort Royal.

From the cathedral tower Charles and his staff had a splendid view of the river meadows, crossed by hedges, south-west of the city, where the Royalists had won two victories during the Civil War. A great deal of imagination is needed to reconstruct the scene today, for the meadows are now all built over.

In his plan for the attack on Worcester Oliver Cromwell broke a vital rule of military strategy, but a general of his genius knows when a rule can be broken. He decided to divide his forces into two parts, which would be separated by a wide river; and to attack from both the western and eastern sides of the Severn. To make this possible he needed two bridges, across the Severn and the Teme at their junction. He sent men southwards down the Severn to collect twenty substantial boats for pontoon bridges. These were collected at Upton-on-Severn, eleven miles south of Worcester.

Cromwell decided to attack Worcester on the 3rd September, a date which heartened his troops, for it was the anniversary of their victory at Dunbar.

Early in the morning of the 3rd September, 1651, King Charles and his staff on the cathedral tower saw the enemy moving into their positions. One half of the Roundhead force, some fifteen thousand men, mostly the less experienced militia, formed up in the meadows to the west of the Severn safely out of cannon and musket range from the city. Half of these faced Fort Royal and the Sidbury Gate; the rest were close to the junction of the two rivers. This force was under the direct command of Cromwell himself. Cannon were brought up to bombard Fort Royal and the Sidbury Gate.

The other half of the Parliament army marched into position on the west bank of the Severn, facing the Teme. No attack was made, however, because eleven miles away, at Upton, soldiers were still laboriously towing twenty boats towards Worcester.

Having seen, probably with some surprise, that Cromwell had divided his forces, King Charles went down from the tower, mounted his horse and rode round his own positions with cheering words for everyone. Some of his men were posted on the walls of the town and a force at Fort Royal guarded the Sidbury Gate. The main part of his infantry were in the meadows on the west bank of the Severn. Their front was protected by the Teme, and their left flank by the Severn. The infantry in these hedge-crossed meadows were in three formations. One was astride the Powick Road, one facing the junction of the rivers, and the third, in reserve, was close to the city walls and near St John's Bridge over the River Severn.

A small Royalist advance guard was posted across the Teme, at the village of Powick, about a mile beyond the Teme. Powick Bridge, the scene of Prince Rupert's success in 1642, had been destroyed, but a temporary construction of planks remained, by which men but not horses could cross. The Royalists in the meadows found good cover behind the hedges dividing the meadows.

The Royalist cavalry were in reserve, behind the city, ready to be brought forward as required. They could ride through the city and out by St John's Gate to the west of the Severn, or by the Sidbury Gate to the eastern side.

The morning passed slowly for the waiting Royalists. The Roundheads made no move, waiting for the boats to come from Upton. It must have been a trying time for the sixteen thousand Scots and the thirty thousand Roundheads, waiting in the bright sunshine for the order to attack. It was not until two o'clock in the afternoon that the men towing the boats came into sight. Very quickly two pontoon bridges were put into position. They were close together, one over the Teme, the other over the Severn, and providing a link joining the two divided parts of the Roundhead army.

At about three o'clock in the afternoon the Roundhead trumpets sounded, colours were raised, and the first move of the attack was made. This was against the Royalist advance guard across the Teme at Powick. This small outpost delayed the enemy as much as possible, and they fell back across the bridge. Some of the few relics of this famous battle are the bullet marks in the tower of Powick church.

The Roundheads fought their way across the Teme, some by the ruined bridge, some by a ford west of Powick, and some by the pontoon bridge. Every foot of ground was hotly disputed by the musket fire of the Scots; but the Roundheads forced their way over the river and the battle was joined in the meadows. It was hard, stubborn and costly fighting. The Scots, pressed back by superior numbers, fought from hedgerow to hedgerow.

Seeing that ground was being gained, Cromwell crossed the Severn from the east bank by the pontoon bridge, taking with him troops to reinforce the attack. It was at this stage of the battle that the young king, not twenty-one years old, showed his generalship. From the cathedral tower he saw that regiments were being withdrawn from the east bank and he saw the chance to make an all-out attack on that side. Hastening down from the cathedral tower, he collected every available man from the city and sent word to David Leslie, commanding the royal cavalry, to bring them forward.

For some reason Leslie refused. We do not know whether it was because he disapproved of the tactics, whether his nerve failed him, or whether it was downright treachery. The fact is that this precious body of two thousand well-armed cavalry stayed where they were, behind the city and out of the battle.

Charles put himself at the head of the troops and, to the ring of trumpets and the roll of drums, with his standard borne beside him, advanced out of the Sidbury Gate. This attack, so sudden and so spirited, caught the Roundheads unawares, and, fighting furiously, they were relentlessly borne back. The success of the battle was in suspense. The guns which had been bombarding Fort Royal were taken, and it seemed that this brilliant counter-attack was going to defeat and scatter half of Cromwell's force.

Cromwell was himself leading his infantry against the stubborn defence on the west bank of the Severn when the news of the alarmingly successful counter-attack on the other side of the Severn was brought to him. He acted instantly. He drew off a part of his troops from the battle among the hedgerows and led them across the Severn by the pontoon bridge. The presence of the

Lord General heartened his retreating regiments, who were mostly militia, and they steadied. Cromwell threw his men against the Royalist right flank, and for an hour or more Royalists and Roundheads were locked in furious battle.

Charles seemed to be everywhere, always in the front of the fight. On one occasion his line was forced back almost to the Sidbury Gate and Charles was himself unhorsed. He leapt on to a mound 'and so encouraged his foot that the enemy retired with loss'.

With that crisis eased, Charles found another horse, and galloped through Worcester to where David Leslie's two thousand horse still stood inactive. He rode up and down their ranks pleading with them to come forward, but, mysteriously, they would not. It is likely that if two thousand fresh cavalry had at that stage ridden through the city and out of the Sidbury Gate the weight of their charge would have had a telling effect on the battle-weary foot of Cromwell.

When the young king rode back through Worcester the tide of battle had turned finally against him. His formations were breaking and, although scattered groups of Royalists fought on desperately, their plight was hopeless. Soon disorganised bands of Royalist soldiers fell back into the city and the Roundheads swept in. Fierce fighting continued in the cobbled streets. Cromwell was victorious. As he said, 'It is, for aught I know, a crowning mercy.'

The battle had been long and hard; 'as stiff a contest for four or five hours as ever I have seen,' wrote Oliver Cromwell in his despatch to the Council of State.

From the moment that Charles crossed the border with his Scottish army, Cromwell had planned every move with unerring judgment. The dramatic race of the two armies down England, edging the invaders to the west, had succeeded as Cromwell had wished. Once the Royalist army was inside Worcester, it was in the trap Cromwell had set. The battle of Worcester was between amateurs and cool efficient professionals. The result was inevitable. The authority of the government of Parliament was not challenged again while Cromwell lived.

King Charles II at the Battle of Worcester, 1651

When it was clear the battle was lost Leslie's cavalry galloped away to the north in the vain hope of escape. The hope was vain because every escape route had been carefully stopped by Round-head cavalry. The fugitives scattered and were remorselessly hunted down. The Royalist foot who survived had even less chance of escape. They, too, were ruthlessly hunted through woodland and moorland.

Cromwell's objective had been two-fold: first to annihilate the Scottish army, and then to capture Charles Stuart. His first pur-pose was most thoroughly achieved, but not the second. Of the hundreds of fugitives who roamed and hid in the countryside around Worcester after the battle, one eluded all efforts to capture him – Charles Stuart.

The ruthlessly efficient army of Parliament hunted the king throughout the west country for six weeks. There was a reward in gold for anyone who captured 'the pretender, Charles Stuart, a dark man more than two yards high'; the penalty for harbouring him was death. Yet he escaped, by means of a series of hair-raising and romantic adventures.

The story of the king hiding in the oak tree at Boscobel is known to all, but that was only one of his adventures. He was dressed as a woodcutter, his face and hands stained with walnut juice; he travelled through troops of Roundheads disguised as a lady's servant; and he hid in secret rooms behind the panelling in country houses. Devoted people of all classes scorned the reward and risked death to help him. It almost seems as if the young man enjoyed the adventures of life and death.

Close though the hunt was, he eluded capture and, at last, six weeks after the battle of Worcester, he slipped away from Brighton in a small boat and landed safely in France. On the 3rd September, 1660, nine years to the day after the battle of Worces-ter, King Charles II returned to England to the ringing of joy bells and the firing of triumphant royal salutes; returned to reign for twenty-five years as king of England.

Note: The full story of the adventures of Charles II after Worcester may be read in the author's *Hunt Royal.*

Chapter 12

'King Monmouth'

The Battle of Sedgemoor

6th July 1685

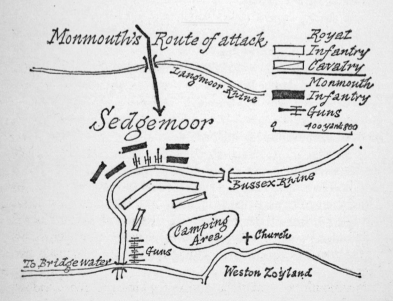

Monmouth's Route of attack

Royal
Infantry
Cavalry

Monmouth
Infantry

Guns

Langmoor Rhine

Sedgemoor

0   400 yards 800

Bussex Rhine

Camping
Area

Church

To Bridgewater

Guns

Weston Zoyland

When King Charles II died in February, 1685, there was no royal prince or princess to succeed him, so his brother, the Duke of York, became King James II (see the family tree on page 143). Three months later, on the 30th May, three ships, a thirty-two-gun frigate and two smaller ones, sailed from Holland for England. This tiny fleet carried three hundred armed men; fifteen hundred swords, pikes and muskets; two hundred barrels of gunpowder, and four small field guns. On board the frigate was James, Duke of Monmouth, sailing to England to wrest the crown of England from his uncle, James II.

The Duke of Monmouth, thirty-six years old in 1685, was a son of King Charles II. His mother was Lucy Walters, a lady from Haverfordwest in Pembrokeshire. King Charles had been fond of young James, and when James was thirteen he recognised him publicly as his son and created him Baron Tyndale, Earl of Doncaster, and Duke of Monmouth, and made him a Knight of the Garter.

The boy, like his father, was handsome and charming, and he was, of course, made much of by the Court. When he grew up he became Captain of the King's Life Guard and Chancellor of Cambridge University. He was a rich, splendid and accomplished young man, and he saw successful active service in Scotland and France.

Monmouth was ambitious, and as the king and queen had no

children he began to think of succeeding his father as king of England. This was not altogether his fault. The king's brother, the Duke of York, was an ardent Roman Catholic. There were five hundred Protestants to every Roman Catholic in England. It was little more than a hundred years since England had broken away from the Roman Catholic Church, and the great majority of Englishmen dreaded coming under its power again. The Parliament side in the Civil War, which had ended only twenty-five years before, had been strongly Puritan, and bitterly opposed to the Church of Rome.

In all these circumstances it was inevitable that there was a very strong feeling against the Roman Catholic Duke of York becoming king of England; indeed, if Charles II had called Parliament in the latter half of his reign, which he steadfastly refused to do, the Duke of York would have been excluded from the succession. Monmouth had been brought up as a Protestant, and many influential people in England considered supporting his claim to the throne, preferring a Protestant king, even though he was not fully of the blood royal, to the Roman Catholic Duke of York.

This situation produced plots while Charles II was still alive, the most famous being the Rye House plot, in which Monmouth was involved. When it was discovered a number of people were executed, but the young duke was pardoned.

Monmouth continued to intrigue until at last his father's patience was exhausted. He was dismissed from his high offices and banished. He went to The Hague in Holland, where he was welcomed by his cousins, William, Prince of Orange, and his wife, the Princess Mary, daughter of the Duke of York.

Intrigues continued in Holland, and a desperate plot was laid. It was arranged that directly Charles II died and his Roman Catholic brother succeeded as James II, Monmouth would go to England and raise his standard as the Protestant champion. At the same time the Earl of Argyll, also in exile in Holland, would go to Scotland and raise Scotland in revolt in Monmouth's name. King Charles died in February, 1685, and in June Monmouth and Argyll sailed for England and Scotland.

The Houses of Stuart and Hanover

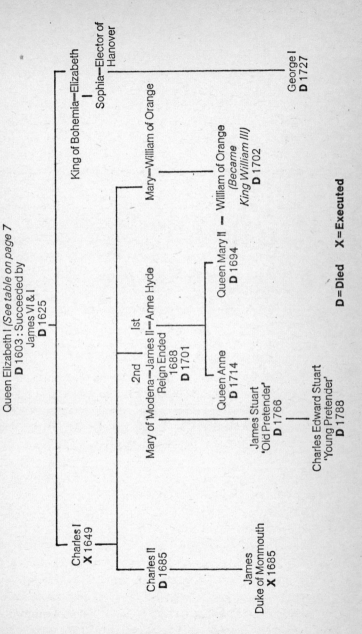

Queen Elizabeth I *(See table on page 7)*
D 1603 : Succeeded by
James VI & I
D 1625

Charles I
X 1649

King of Bohemia—Elizabeth

Sophia—Elector of Hanover

George I
D 1727

Mary—William of Orange

Queen Mary II **=** William of Orange
D 1694   *(Became King William III)*
                      D 1702

2nd   1st
Mary of Modena—James II—Anne Hyde
Reign Ended
1688
D 1701

Queen Anne
D 1714

Charles II
D 1685

James Stuart
'Old Pretender'
D 1766

Charles Edward Stuart
'Young Pretender'
D 1788

James
Duke of Monmouth
X 1685

D = Died   **X** = Executed

These plots and moves were not unknown to James II. The country militia was called out throughout England and began to assemble in market towns. The fleet was at sea on the look-out for an invasion force.

Monmouth's three ships escaped detection, however, but contrary winds drove them south, and it was only after a voyage of twelve days that they were able to land in England. They put in at the little harbour of Lyme in Dorset, and as soon as he stepped ashore the Duke of Monmouth fell on his knees to thank God for his safe arrival and to ask His help in the great adventure that lay ahead.

The town council of Lyme were thoroughly alarmed at the sight of the three ships. They at once met and wondered whether or not they should fire their one cannon at the invaders. The problem was solved when somebody pointed out that they had no gunpowder. So they did the next best thing; they ordered the drum to be beaten to call the dozen or so militia in the town to arms. For some reason or other – perhaps it was prudence – only one turned up. He went down to the harbour and joined the Duke of Monmouth.

Meanwhile, Monmouth's men had disembarked, and the stores, ammunition and the four guns were unloaded. Monmouth led his small force up the steep path from the harbour to the town, and was welcomed joyously by the people of Lyme. All the able-bodied men, young and old, turned out and joined him.

In the market place Monmouth set up his standard, blue and gold with the motto 'Fear none but God'. He was proclaimed the true son and heir of the late King Charles II. The proclamation declared that King James had set fire to London and had poisoned his brother the king, and the simple country folk believed these outrageous lies. Monmouth was declared to be the 'Head and Captain General of the Protestant Forces of the Kingdom'. This call to the sturdy Protestant belief of the west countrymen, coupled with Monmouth's handsome and splendid appearance, brought men hurrying to his standard from the countryside around. Monmouth did not then claim the title of king, but his excited followers called him 'King Monmouth'.

Unfortunately for Monmouth, though the labourers, shepherds and miners flocked to his standard, the gentry and yeomen farmers stayed away. His army, which grew so rapidly, was perilously short of officers. The gentry were as strongly Protestant as the others, but they were less impetuous. King James had only been on the throne for four months and he had given no indication that the Protestant faith was in any danger. Moreover, they did not have much faith in Monmouth's ability. So they stayed at home, and when Monmouth marched to Taunton his army of three thousand untrained and undisciplined men lacked leaders.

They also lacked arms. The few weapons Monmouth had brought with him could only equip a fraction of his force. The rest were armed only with scythes and hedging hooks. But Monmouth's men marched proudly northwards, ready to fight and, if needs be, die for the Protestant cause and their Protestant 'King Monmouth'.

Monmouth entered Taunton in triumph; girls strewed flowers before him and the church bells rang joyously. On the 20th June Monmouth was proclaimed King James II, the same title as his uncle. So enthusiastic were the people of Taunton and the country around that four thousand men joined him there, but still very few of the gentry came forward. At Taunton Monmouth obtained much needed weapons and powder, military stores and baggage wagons.

His first objective was Bristol, which throughout the Civil War had been strongly Puritan. If he could capture Bristol he would have a substantially fortified headquarters, ample supply of stores and ammunition, and a valuable port; it would, indeed, be the ideal base for his further movements, which, of course, would end in London.

With his army increased and slightly better equipped, he marched to Bridgwater, where, again, he was received with delirious joy. He embodied more recruits in his army, and marched on through Glastonbury to Wells.

At this stage of the invasion, events began to go against him. The first was the weather, for unusually heavy rains soon covered the rough roads with mud and made movement difficult. The other trouble was the presence at his rear and on his flanks of two squadrons of regular horse commanded by a brilliant young officer, Colonel Lord Churchill. He had been given the task of keeping the rebel column under observation and harrying it whenever possible while the main royal army was brought up. It was unfortunate for Monmouth that these squadrons should be commanded by one of the very greatest soldiers England has produced, for Lord Churchill became, twenty years later, the Duke of Marlborough, victor of Blenheim, Ramillies, Oudenarde and Malplaquet.

The presence of Lord Churchill's squadrons and the news of other royal squadrons between Wells and Bristol checked Monmouth, and he changed his plans and marched to Bath. But the gates of the city were closed against him. The messenger he sent under a white flag was promptly shot.

With Bristol barred from him by King James's army, and with Bath defiant, Monmouth could go no farther forward. He had reached the limit of his invasion. He turned about and marched back, southwards to Frome. Here he received the news that the Earl of Argyll had been captured and executed in Edinburgh. The whole audacious venture now depended on Monmouth and his peasant army. His dreams had begun to crumble, and he was melancholy as he led his men back through Shepton Mallett, Wells and Glastonbury to Bridgwater.

When King James had received the news of Monmouth's landing at Lyme Regis he acted quickly. Nine of the eleven regiments which then formed the standing army were ordered to meet at Salisbury. The commander-in-chief was Lord Feversham, a French Protestant nobleman who had become a naturalised Englishman twenty years before. Feversham had military experience in active service on the Continent, but this was his first independent command. Colonel Lord Churchill was his second-in-command.

When Monmouth marched back into Bridgwater on the 4th July, the royal army was at Somerton, fourteen miles south-east of Bridgwater and eight south of Glastonbury. The army was camped here when a messenger brought the news that Monmouth had halted in Bridgwater. This seemed to be the opportunity Feversham was waiting for, and the next day he marched to Langport, and on up the Bridgwater road to Weston Zoyland only three-and-a-half miles south-east of Bridgwater.

Feversham made camp at Weston Zoyland, where there was a natural defence round the village in the form of a deep, wide drain. This, the Bussex Rhine, ran along the north of the village, and then turned southwards covering the western boundary. To the north of the village stretches a flat low-lying peat moor, known as Sedgemoor.

Feversham had chosen a good position for his army to spend the night, for not only was it protected by the Bussex Rhine, but there was another deep ditch a mile to the north, in front of the position, the Langmoor Rhine; these two ditches were to play a vital part in the battle of Sedgemoor.

The royal army consisted of seven hundred cavalry, eighteen hundred infantry, and seventeen guns. In Bridgwater, three-and-a-half miles away, the Duke of Monmouth had eight hundred cavalry, two thousand nine hundred infantry, and four guns. Thus the royal army was inferior in quantity to the rebels, but in quality it was immensely superior. Monmouth commanded an army of untrained and ill-equipped countrymen. Feversham commanded nine regiments of well-equipped, regular soldiers, properly officered.

This was the first occasion on which the British Army, which had been formed twenty-four years before by King Charles II, marched together on active service; the beginning of a tradition which was to stretch ahead through our history. Only two regiments of the army of those days were absent on service elsewhere, the Scots Guards and the Buffs. The regiments which encamped at Weston Zoyland and which were to fight the battle of

Sedgemoor the next morning were, to give the titles under which
they were later known:

Cavalry
> The Life Guards, the Royal Horse Guards, and the Royal
> Dragoons.

Infantry
> The Grenadier Guards (two battalions), the Coldstream
> Guards, the Royal Scots, the King's Own, and the Queen's
> Royal Regiment.

Feversham posted a careful ring of outposts round his camp at
Weston Zoyland, including a strong patrol of Life Guards, under
Colonel Oglethorpe, based on the village of Bawdrip, four miles
north of Weston Zoyland. This force was to patrol the two roads
north of Bridgwater so that Feversham would know at once if
Monmouth marched out towards Bristol again. The seventeen
royalist guns were sited to the west of Weston Zoyland by the
side of the Bridgwater road, to cover it against attack. The tents
of the infantry were pitched to the north of the village, about a
hundred yards short of the Bussex Rhine.

At eleven o'clock that night Lord Feversham rode round his
outposts to make sure they were all in the right positions and
watchful. He had a word with all the commanders, and, confident
that his camp was properly protected, he rode back to the village
and, at two o'clock went to bed in a cottage. All was quiet; the
moor was veiled in mist, and Feversham looked forward to several
hours' sleep. In fact, he was to have only half an hour.

The Duke of Monmouth had spent a melancholy day in Bridgwater. His plan to capture Bristol had failed, and Bath would have
none of him. His troops were dispirited at the retreat: they had
been marching for four days in heavy rain, and their boots were
worn through. Monmouth was tempted to give up the whole
venture and ride away with two or three friends and find a ship
to take him to France.

There was, however, another possibility, to march quickly
northwards into Gloucestershire and Cheshire. If he could get a

Monmouth's night march to Sedgemoor, 1685

good start on his enemy there was a chance of finding strong support in those two counties in the name of the Protestant cause.

Eventually this plan was decided on, and on the evening of the 5th July Monmouth's army was mustered in Bridgwater preparatory to marching out. The horses were harnessed to the baggage wagons, and all preparations made. The Duke of Monmouth was riding across the old bridge from the castle into Bridgwater when he met a farm worker named Richard Godfrey.

Richard Godfrey's master farmed at Chedzoy, about two miles north of Weston Zoyland. During the afternoon the farmer had climbed the tower of Chedzoy church and had watched the royalist army setting up their camp. He had also seen and noted the position of Feversham's outposts. Being well disposed towards the Protestant rebellion, he had sent his man Godfrey to give this information to the Duke of Monmouth. Godfrey also told the Duke that, although the road to Weston Zoyland was covered by guns, there was a safe way round by which the royal army could be surprised. Godfrey offered to lead Monmouth across Sedgemoor by this safe route.

Monmouth immediately climbed the church tower in Bridgwater to see for himself. With a telescope he could see the tents of the royal army at Weston Zoyland. Here, after all, was a chance of success. If he could achieve that most difficult of military operations, a long night march in silence, he might be able to catch his enemy unawares, and kill the royalist troops in their beds or as they ran about in panic. It was true that the militia was under arms throughout the country, but many of them were well disposed towards Monmouth. Lord Feversham had fifteen hundred of the Wiltshire militia with him, but he was so unsure of their loyalty that he had made them camp three miles to the rear of Weston Zoyland.

His melancholy gone, the Duke of Monmouth summoned a council of war. The question was raised whether the royal army was entrenched. Richard Godfrey was sent to find out. He returned, having travelled some seven miles there and back, with the news that there was no sign of any digging. The council of war thereupon decided to make the night attack.

At eleven o'clock that night, the 5th July, 1685, Monmouth's army marched off on its great enterprise. Spirits were now high. After their bitter disappointments they were going to wrest the victory in a most dramatic manner; the royalist army was to be slain, swiftly and mercilessly. 'We shall have little more to do than lock the stable doors, and seize the troopers in their beds,' they said.

As they would have to march close to enemy patrols absolute silence was essential. The order was passed that no drum was to beat and no pistol was to be fired. If any man spoke he was to be stabbed immediately by his neighbours. The password was 'Soho', the counter-sign 'Monmouth and God with us'.

Richard Godfrey led the way. The army left Bridgwater on the Bristol road, the infantry – musketeers and scythesmen – leading, then the eight hundred horse under Lord Grey and the four guns bringing up the rear. Two and a half miles from Bridgwater the army halted and the baggage wagons were left with a small guard and one of the guns, ready to continue the march to Bristol when the battle had been won. Godfrey then led the army eastwards, and then swung south to bypass the village of Bawdrip, where Colonel Oglethorpe's Life Guards were based. There was another halt, and the ammunition wagons were left at a farm, the musketeers and gunners having been given a full issue of powder and ball.

Godfrey now turned due south, leading the army across Sedgemoor towards Weston Zoyland. A cavalry patrol was heard approaching, and the long column halted and stood silent. The patrol rode by with a jingle of harness and creak of leather, quite unaware. The column marched on, passing quite close to a patrol of Royalist horse in the village of Chedzoy. The next halt was at Langmoor Rhine, which crossed Sedgemoor about a mile north of the enemy camp.

There was a long and anxious wait while Richard Godfrey looked for the ford of stepping stones which crossed this ditch.

When at last he found it, the cavalry took the lead, Lord Grey leading them across. Monmouth must have been well pleased, for all was going as he had hoped. There remained only a mile of Sedgemoor between him and the enemy sleeping in their tents at Weston Zoyland. Then suddenly, as the last of the cavalry was crossing the ditch, came the sound of a pistol shot, fired at Grey's horse by a Royalist trooper on patrol.

The precious and vital element of surprise was lost. Monmouth had to act quickly; the slow silent approach had to be abandoned. He must strike before the enemy had time to beat to arms. He ordered Grey to lead his cavalry forward, cross the Bussex Rhine and attack the enemy on the flanks. Meanwhile, Monmouth would bring the foot forward as fast as he could to attack in front.

Grey put himself at the head of his eight hundred horsemen and led them forward at the canter. Monmouth's men marched briskly. Success was still possible, for it takes time even for the most disciplined troops to get into position from their beds and ready for action.

The rebel cavalry trotted briskly forward through the mist until they were stopped by the Bussex Rhine. They could not find the crossing places without a guide, and Godfrey had been left behind. They divided into two, one half riding to the left and the other to the right, seeking crossing places.

Sir Francis Compton, commanding the King's cavalry outpost in Chedzoy, heard the pistol shot and acted quickly. He assembled his hundred and fifty horse and led them back across the moor to the Royalist camp. But first he had sent off a trooper at the gallop to raise the alarm in the camp. This man reined-in at the Bussex Rhine and shouted his dramatic news at the tents a hundred yards away. Soon he was answered, and the sharp commanding rattle of a drum was heard.

Other drums began to sound, beating 'To Arms'. The royal foot scrambled from their beds and hurried to fall in, hastened by the harsh commands of the N.C.Os. Officers came hurrying from their tents, buckling on their swords, and gradually, out of the chaos, the lines were formed and the regiments stood ready.

Colonel Churchill was quickly on the scene, posting the regiments in line along the ditch until Lord Feversham, called by his servant after a bare half-hour of sleep, took command.

The rebel horse on the far side of the Bussex Rhine desperately sought crossing places. If they could only get at the enemy infantry while they were still half awake and their ranks still unformed, victory might still be possible. The horse which had turned left-handed did find a crossing, but they were too late. Compton's horse were already there. They had crossed the ditch and stood denying the crossing to the rebels. There was a brisk engagement, and the rebels were driven off.

The rest of Grey's horse were challenged suddenly by a regiment forming up.

'Who are you for?' came the challenge.

'The king!' was the reply.

'Which king?'

'King Monmouth, God with him!' The answer was shouted defiantly at the invisible challenger.

The reply was short and to the point. 'Then take *that* with you!' And a volley was fired.

The roar and the flash of muskets and the deathly hail of bullets terrified the horses. They were not trained cavalry mounts, but moorland horses taken into service by Monmouth during his advance. The horses were as untrained and inexperienced as the men who rode them.

The whole body galloped away into the mist in terror, and many of them dashed right into the ranks of the advancing rebel foot. These, hearing cavalry charging down on them through the mist, naturally thought they were the enemy, and opened fire. This second attack broke the nerve of horses and riders completely and they galloped away into the darkness, scattering wildly; away out of the battle.

Thus the Duke of Monmouth had lost his cavalry. They were to have charged on the flank of the enemy, cutting them down, so that the infantry could march in and clinch the matter. Monmouth had only his foot soldiers now, and these he formed from column into line, three regiments in front and two behind. They halted about a hundred yards from the Bussex Rhine, and would go no farther. They stood closely together, shoulder to shoulder, and began firing into the darkness. It was the natural conduct of untrained men, but quite useless. The muskets were aimed too high and though the noise and the smell of the powder may have heartened the rebels little harm was done to the royal infantry lined up on the other side of the ditch. These wisely held their fire until dawn should show them their enemy.

Damage was done, however, by Monmouth's three guns which were brought into action alongside the infantry. They caused casualties to the infantry opposite them, but the regiments stood fast with admirable discipline.

Feversham's guns, it will be remembered, were sited to the west of Weston Zoyland, covering the Bridgwater road, some five hundred yards from the infantry position at the Bussex Rhine. When the rebel guns opened fire, the royal guns were urgently called for to reply. But there was disorder at the royal guns. First the drivers could not be found, and when they were roused from their billets they could not find where the horses were stabled.

The scene of shouting and swearing was resolved in a remarkable way. The Bishop of Winchester was with the royal army, and he had once been a soldier. He rose to the occasion by bringing round his own coach horses and traces. With these the guns were hurriedly brought into action and quickly silenced Monmouth's three small cannon.

Then a cry began to go up from the rebel infantry. 'Ammunition, ammunition! For the Lord's sake, more ammunition!' But none came. Some of Grey's terrified cavalry had ridden past the ammunition wagons, a mile to the rear, and they caught the panic and galloped away. So the musket fire from the rebel foot became intermittent, as they waited, like their enemy, for the dawn.

With the first gleam of morning Lord Feversham rode across the Bussex Rhine to look at the situation. Monmouth's foot still stood in their close ranks, firing desultorily with their last powder and ball. To the everlasting honour of these countrymen, they never seemed to consider retreat, still believing that when the enemy showed himself they could fight it out. Feversham's plan was simple. Colonel Oglethorpe had returned from Bawdrip with his cavalry, Sir Francis Compton was there with his, and the cavalry which had remained in the camp had long been mounted and formed up. Feversham ordered the cavalry to attack the two flanks of the rebel foot.

The sight of two hundred horses charging is terrifying; the more so when they are mounted by skilled and determined swordsmen. Yet the West Country men and lads stood firm, fighting back valiantly with their scythes and bill-hooks and clubbed muskets. Time after time the cavalry were driven back, and as men fell the ranks closed. For a time the Duke of Monmouth fought with his men, pike in hand. But as the sky lightened with the dawn he stood apart, troubled by a great decision which had to be made: to stay and die fighting with his devoted men, or to escape while he could, perhaps to fight another day, perhaps only to save his life?

It would have been better for his good name if he had decided to stay. But he took off his armour, mounted his horse, and, with a few companions, rode away north-eastwards towards the Polden Hills. There is a legend that in his flight he jumped a seventeen-foot ditch.

As full daylight came, Lord Feversham watched the hard fight between his cavalry and the doomed square of rebel infantry, waiting for the moment to go in to the 'kill'. Then, as he himself wrote, 'The pikes of one of their battalions began to shake, and at last open.' He ordered his six battalions of infantry to fix bayonets and cross the ditch. They formed up on the other side and charged. At the same moment the cavalry, which had withdrawn for the purpose, charged yet again on both flanks of the rebel square.

These gallant countrymen had reached the limit of their endurance, and, charged by fresh troops from the front, and by cavalry on both flanks, they at last broke. One battalion – or, rather, its pathetic remnants – withdrew together six hundred yards to a cornfield and there, among the high standing corn, they fought it out to the very end. As the others fled across Sedgemoor they were shot down, ridden down or overtaken and bayoneted. Those who managed to hide among the corn or in ditches were ruthlessly hunted out and killed, some with sword or bayonet, many by being hanged on the nearest tree.

Five hundred prisoners, many of them wounded, were packed into Weston Zoyland church; no surgeons went to attend to their wounds, no food or water was allowed to be taken to them. A long line of prisoners was taken to Bridgwater, their hands tied together like slaves, and a score or more were hanged forthwith. Some were hanged in chains, to starve to death.

Monmouth escaped into Hampshire and hid in the wild country of the New Forest. He exchanged clothes with a country labourer, who was caught and so narrowed the hunt. After two days they hunted him down in a field of standing corn. He was so ragged and pathetic when they caught him that they could not believe it was the great Duke. But in his pocket they found the gold and diamond Order of the Garter his father, King Charles, had given him twenty years before.

Monmouth was taken to London, guarded by a whole regiment of infantry. He made abject appeals for mercy to his uncle, King James II, but there could be no mercy for such rank high treason. On the 15th July, only nine days after the battle, Monmouth was executed on Tower Hill.

Sedgemoor was the last battle fought on English soil. More than two thousand of Monmouth's men were slain in battle, hundreds more afterwards. The royal army lost only four hundred, killed and wounded.

The savagery of the vengeance taken by King James II is a stain on our history. The infamous Judge Jefferies travelled the west country on what was came to be known as 'the Bloody Assize'. He went from town to town, trying those accused of taking part in the rebellion, and few who were accused escaped his savage sentence. Three hundred and thirty men and women were hanged, eight hundred and fifty-five were transported for life to the West Indies, to live as slaves. It is small consolation to know that in 1689, when William III succeeded James II, Judge Jefferies was arrested and died miserably in the Tower of London.

Chapter 13

King William or King James?

The Battle of the Boyne

1st July 1690

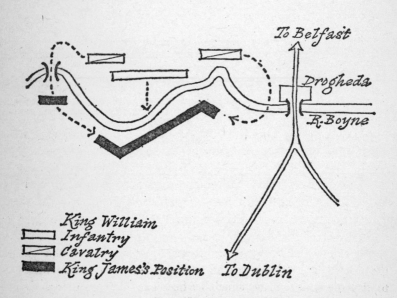

The battle of the Boyne was not long in suspense, and the casualties were not heavy; yet the results were far-reaching. When the armies of King William and King James faced each other across the River Boyne on that July morning in 1690 the fate of Europe hung in the balance.

The battle between rival kings of England, James II and William III, was for much more than the crown of England. It was a vital conflict between the Roman Catholic and the Protestant faiths, and all Europe was anxiously concerned in the outcome. To understand the importance of the battle of the Boyne we must find out how it came to be fought in Ireland, and we must tell the story of the siege of Londonderry the year before, for the siege was the prelude to the battle.

In 1685, as we have read, James II crushed the Monmouth rebellion at the battle of Sedgemoor. The country folk of the west of England fought for Monmouth because he put himself up as the Protestant champion. The country generally failed to support Monmouth because King James, although a Roman Catholic, had shown no sign of interfering with the Protestant faith in the few months he had been on the throne.

When the rebellion was put down, however, James enlarged the army to increase his power, and began to show his intention to dispense with the laws which has been passed to ensure that the country remained Protestant. The Dissenters, or extreme

Protestants, were persecuted. Roman Catholic officers were appointed second-in-command in every regiment, so that the king only had to dismiss the colonels to have his army commanded by Catholics.

Roman Catholics were appointed to important posts in the government and in the church. In many ways the king made it clear that he intended to restore his realm to the Church of Rome. England was essentially Protestant and there was great unrest and secret plotting in high places.

In 1688 two events brought matters to a head: the Declaration of Indulgence and the birth of a son to the king. The Declaration of Indulgence promised 'lenient treatment' to any Roman Catholic charged with breaking the laws which existed against them, so that in effect full rights were restored to them. They were allowed to hold office in the government, in the church or in the Army or Navy, in spite of the fact that this was expressly forbidden by law.

The birth of the prince meant that King James would probably be succeeded by another Roman Catholic. In the seventeenth century religion was a very live topic in men's minds, and Protestant England saw that drastic action must be taken to remove King James from the throne. Secret letters passed between London and The Hague, the capital of Holland, and William, Prince of Orange, was invited to invade England to win the crown from James.

William had a double claim to the English crown (see the family tree on page 143). He was a grandson of King Charles I and he was married to Princess Mary, a daughter of James II. Even more important, both William and Mary were staunch Protestants. William accepted the invitation and landed in England with an army of English and Dutch regiments. This time it was not only the simple country folk who rallied to the standard of the Protestant champion; noblemen, squires, merchants and yeomen joined him. Some senior officers of the army of King James went over to William. Whole regiments were ready to go as well.

William marched to London, to be joyfully received by all,

and James fled to France. Parliament declared the throne vacant and begged William and Mary to become king and queen. Thus King James II was replaced in England by King William III and Queen Mary II.

King James was welcomed by Louis XIV of France. This highly intelligent and powerful king saw how he could use James to further his designs for becoming the master of Europe. He supplied money and an army, and James sailed for Ireland. The plan was simple: Ireland was strongly Roman Catholic and it would be, it seemed, easy for James to subdue the Protestant minority. Louis would attack Holland and William would naturally go to rescue his homeland. When King William and his army were in Holland James could cross from Ireland and regain his crown. England would become Roman Catholic, its king the vassal of Louis of France. Thus Louis, with England under his thumb, would soon become master of Europe.

It was this far-reaching strategy which was finally settled at the battle of the Boyne on the 1st July, 1690. But the Boyne was the climax of a twelve-month campaign in Ireland, in which James, with his French and Irish army, tried in vain to subdue the Irish Protestants. At the first stage of the campaign was the epic siege of Londonderry.

While the majority of the Irish were Roman Catholic there were many Protestants, Irish, English and Scottish, in Ireland. Most of them lived in the north, as they still do. The principal stronghold was the country around the city of Londonderry in the extreme north. When James marched north from Dublin at the head of a strong Irish and French army, most of the Protestants around Londonderry went into the city.

Londonderry was a new city, built on the ruins of Derry, which had been burned to the ground seventy years before. The new city was renamed Londonderry as a compliment to London, whose merchants provided much of the money for the rebuilding.

The Governor of Londonderry, Robert Lundy, had sent secret word to James promising to surrender as soon as his army arrived. James marched on Londonderry in April 1689, but at the last moment the citizens discovered the treachery of their Governor, and turned him out of office. A new Governor was appointed, and the seven thousand men in Londonderry formed themselves into seven regiments and appointed their own officers.

King James was astonished when guns on the walls, and hastily mounted on the cathedral tower, opened fire. The Irish army made camp out of range of the guns and considered the situation while the men of Londonderry toiled to make the best they could of the inadequate defences. The walls were low and grass-grown, the gates were rusty, the moat was empty, and the drawbridges could not be raised. It seemed madness to try to defend Londonderry, which was ill-stocked with ammunition and food, against the army of thirty thousand.

The next day King James sent Lord Strabane, a man of high reputation in Ireland, under a flag of truce. The commander of one of the new regiments, Colonel Murray, went out of the gate to meet Lord Strabane. Strabane told Murray that the citizens of Londonderry should have a free pardon for all that was past if they would submit to their lawful sovereign, while Murray himself should have a colonel's commission in the king's army and a thousand pounds in cash.

Murray's answer was memorable. 'My lord,' he said, 'the men of Londonderry have done nothing that requires a pardon, and own no sovereign but King William and Queen Mary. It would not be safe for your lordship to stay here longer, or to come back on the same errand. Pray let me have the honour of seeing you through the lines.'

The conquest of Londonderry seemed an easy matter. King James at once attacked, first bombarding the city from close range, and then mounting determined assaults. Every attack was thrown back, and the men of Londonderry sallied out in violent counter-attacks. Their watchword was 'No surrender'. When the small supply of cannon balls was expended they made new ones from bricks coated with lead.

After a week of hard fighting around the walls of Londonderry James decided to conquer the city by starving it out. Positions were dug all round the walls and guns were sited on each bank of Lough Foyle, and a heavy boom was thrown across the river to prevent supplies being brought by ship.

It was only their almost superhuman determination which enabled the people of Londonderry to endure the next three months. When their supplies of food were exhausted they ate the horses, and then the dogs. A dog's paw was worth five and six-pence. The daily ration became a little tallow wax and a piece of salted animal skin to chew. Inevitably epidemics broke out, and ten died of sickness for every one killed by a bullet. By July the seven thousand defenders were reduced to three thousand, but they held on; still the watchword was 'No surrender'.

Then one day a sentinel on the cathedral tower sighted the sails of thirty ships in Lough Foyle; ships from England bearing troops, ammunition and, far and away the most important, food. But they came no nearer, they lay at anchor, their masts visible from Londonderry, baulked by the heavy boom across the river. They stayed there, idle, for three weeks. With succour so near and yet so far, the resolution of the brave men and women and children of Londonderry was sorely taxed. The day came when even the meagre ration of tallow and skin could last only two days more. The end was in sight.

Then it was that the master of the merchant ship *Mount Joy* volunteered to run the gauntlet of the guns and try to break the boom. He was a Londonderry man and his ship was loaded with food from London. The master of the *Phoenix*, with a cargo of meal from Scotland, volunteered to go with him. Permission was given, and the *Dartmouth*, a thirty-six-gun frigate, was ordered to escort them. So at sunset on the 28th July the sentinels in Londonderry saw the sails of the three vessels coming down Lough Foyle. The guns lining the banks opened fire as the merchantmen sailed slowly in. The terrible suspense of the people of Londonderry, watching from the walls, can be imagined; the slow approach of the brave sails, the flash and roar of the Irish guns firing at the easy prey, the great questions – could they survive, and could they break the boom?

The tide was low and the only navigable channel ran close to the bank. The *Dartmouth* fired broadside after broadside at the Irish guns and manœuvred to draw the enemy fire to herself. As the little squadron approached the beam the *Mount Joy* took the lead and sailed full-tilt at the obstacle. The huge barricade cracked under the impact and gave way, but the shock drove the *Mount Joy* back on to a mudbank. The Irish yelled with triumph and rushed to their boats to capture the stranded ship. But the *Dartmouth* bore up and scattered them with a broadside of grape-shot.

Meanwhile the *Phoenix* sailed straight for the breach the *Mount Joy* had made, and, to a rending of timbers, and after a moment of anguished doubt, she sailed through. The frigate stood by the *Mount Joy*, protecting her until the rising tide refloated her and she, too, sailed through the gap and anchored with the *Phoenix* at the Londonderry quay.

The bells of the cathedral rang out and the guns on the walls roared defiantly as they fired into the Irish camp; as always, the greatest noise came from 'Roaring Meg', a gun still preserved on the walls of Londonderry in memory of the great siege. Everyone not on duty at the walls was at the quay, eagerly unloading the cargoes of the gallant *Mount Joy* and *Phoenix*. They rolled ashore barrels of meal, six thousand bushels of it. Then came great cheeses, casks of beef, flitches of bacon, kegs of butter, sacks of peas and biscuit, barrels of brandy. While the survivors of the siege feasted, the walls of Londonderry were ringed with bonfires. The rest of the fleet in Lough Foyle was making ready to sail in at dawn.

Three days later the Irish broke camp and marched away. The siege had lasted a hundred and five days. Against all odds, Londonderry had been saved and now, reinforced from England, the Protestants marched southwards, clearing the northern counties of the French and Irish.

The civil war in Ireland continued. King James had his Court and Parliament in Dublin, and passed laws and signed proclamations as king of England, declaring that William and Mary were usurpers whom he would drive from his realm of England.

In August an army of English and Dutch regiments was sent to northern Ireland under the veteran commander, Count Schomberg. The civil war continued in a desultory fashion, with no marked success for either side. In the spring of 1690 William left Lord Marlborough in command of the army in Flanders to go to Ireland himself.

He landed at Carrickfergus, ten miles north of Belfast, on the 14th June, 1690, to the firing of a royal salute. This was repeated by guns placed at intervals along the road so that within an hour of his landing Protestant Ireland knew that King William himself had come. That night a bonfire blazed on every hill-top. Once and for all the question would be settled: King William or King James; Protestant or Roman Catholic. William went at once to Belfast and, ten days later, his army was complete.

King James had thirty thousand men in the field, about two-thirds Irish and one-third French. Every soldier of King James wore a white ribbon in his hat or helmet, in compliment to Louis XIV. King James was financed by French gold, and his army marched under two standards, the Royal Stuart standard, and the Fleur-de-Lis of France.

King William took the field with thirty-six thousand men, half of whom were English. They included many great and famous regiments – the Life Guards, the Blues, and the First Dragoon Guards, and among the infantry, to give them their modern titles, the Scots Guards, the Northumberland Fusiliers, and the Royal Warwickshire Regiment. The other half of the Protestant army consisted of Irish Protestant regiments, Scottish regiments, and regiments from six other countries. There were French Protestants, Dutch, Danish and German troops, and regiments from Luxemburg and Finland.

This army of 'united nations' emphasised that the war was not only to decide who was to be king of England; it was to decide whether Protestant Europe was to remain Protestant. The Protestant countries had all sent their best men and their best officers, all willing to serve under the standard of William of Orange, king of England.

William was eager to bring the enemy to action as soon as possible, and he set off south towards Dublin without delay. The army marched to the lilting, teasing tune of 'Lilliburlero', which ever since has been associated by the Protestants of Ireland with King William and the battle of the Boyne. It was a tune, they said, which danced a king out of three kingdoms.

For three days James's advance guard fell back before William until they reached the River Boyne, twenty miles north of Dublin. The Boyne, a broad river, enters the sea where the city of Drogheda stands. James crossed the Boyne and turned to await William on the south bank. The river bank was entrenched, and the main part of his army was concealed behind hedges and folds in the land.

King William was delighted when, very early in the morning of the 30th June, 1690, he topped a rise and saw the wide valley of the Boyne before him and his enemy in position on the farther bank. He saw with relief that the matter would soon be put to the test of battle. He gave orders for his army to halt and bivouac, and he himself, with a glittering cavalcade of officers, rode along the north bank of the river, examining the situation. That done, he dismounted and called for the sumpter mules. By the side of the river, in the bright sunshine of a fine summer's morning, William and his staff had a picnic breakfast.

This was not unobserved by the Irish on the other bank of the river, and two cannon were secretly brought into position behind a hedge. The picnic breakfast was finished and the officers mounted. Suddenly the cannon opened fire. The first shot killed the horse of Prince George of Denmark, and the second, ricocheting off the ground, struck King William on the right shoulder. He fell forward on his horse's neck. The consternation among the staff can be well imagined.

Word was at once sent back to King James that William had been killed. Messengers galloped back to Dublin. All the bells of the city rang in triumph and people danced in the streets. A frigate set sail for France, and a mud-splashed messenger took the news to the French Court. At eleven o'clock at night soldiers ran

William III leading his cavalry across the Boyne, 1690

through the streets of Paris knocking everyone up. Every house was at once illuminated, tables were set up in the streets, wine was free, and Paris rejoiced that the enemy to the Church of Rome had been killed.

But William was not seriously hurt. His shoulder was bruised, and the flesh torn. A plaster was applied, and he rode back through the lines, to show the cheering troops that all was well.

Throughout the day of the 30th June the guns of both armies were in action. King William's plan of battle was simple and daring, so daring that the elderly and much experienced General Schomberg protested strongly at the risk. It was to make a direct frontal attack with his infantry across the River Boyne, which at that time of the year was shallow enough to be crossed on foot. At the same time, his cavalry were to ride east and west, across the river and attack the enemy on the flanks. For identification – very necessary in an army of so many nationalities – every soldier was to wear a twig with green leaves in his helmet.

The dawn on the 1st July, 1690, was bright and clear, promising a hot day. At four in the morning, William's army was ready. The right wing of his cavalry, commanded by a son of General Schomberg, rode several miles up the river bank and attacked the bridge of Slane, which was guarded by a regiment of Irish dragoons. After a fierce engagement the Irish dragoons were beaten back and William's cavalry crossed the river.

King William himself led the left wing of the cavalry eastwards nearly to Drogheda, and led his squadrons into the water. It was deeper here, being nearer the mouth of the river, and the banks were boggy. They floundered through soft mud into the river, under fire from the south bank. In some places the horses had to swim, but, difficult though it was, William led the squadrons across and they fought their way up on the southern bank and on to dry land.

Meanwhile, the long lines of infantry marched down to the river, drums and fifes leading the twenty thousand men to the lilt of 'Lilliburlero'. The regiments marched shoulder to shoulder – English, Irish, Scottish, French, Dutch, Germans, Luxemburgers and Finns. The drums stopped and they marched into the river. In many places the water was up to the men's armpits and they held their weapons high. For half a mile the waters of the Boyne were alive with muskets and pikes, and everywhere, green twigs.

The Irish made no move until William's infantry were in mid-stream. Then, with wild shouts and the beating of drums, they rose from their trenches, and sprang into action. The surface of the Boyne through which the Protestant infantry were wading became turbulent with cannon ball and musket shot. The infantry continued to wade forward resolutely, and the leading regiments began to climb on to the south bank, formed up again and advanced.

Then an astonishing thing happened. A panic seized the Irish infantry and, throwing away arms, colours and cloaks, they fled towards the hills. Their officers tried desperately to stop them, but to no avail. More than a third of James's infantry ran from the field without firing a shot.

The Irish cavalry and the French infantry did their utmost to compensate for the disaster by fighting magnificently. In many places Irish cavalry regiments rode into the river and fought the Protestant infantry as they waded across. French infantry charged down to the river bank and fought fiercely hand-to-hand with William's men as they were forming up after the crossing. So impetuous was the attack of the Irish cavalry and the French infantry that for half-an-hour the issue was in doubt. But the Protestant regiments stubbornly held their position on the river bank as the line ebbed and flowed in the din and confusion of battle.

Relief came for William's hard-pressed infantry when the squadrons of cavalry came down on the enemy's flanks. Then it was the turn of the French and Irish to hang on grimly to their ground. It was when the day was still undecided that King William rode into the battle, at the head of the squadrons he had led across the river. He rode into the thick of the battle, encouraging his troops. He cantered up to the head of the Enniskillen regiment, who had been driven back by a very gallant and impetuous charge by Irish dragoons. William was not immediately recognised, for his clothes were soaked and stained with mud, and a trooper took him for an enemy and raised his musket to fire. William rode up to him and put aside the carbine.

'What,' he said, 'do you not know your friend?'

The colonel of the Enniskillen shouted, 'It is His Majesty!' The regiment shouted with joy.

'Gentlemen,' said William, 'you shall be my guards today. I have heard much of you. Now let me see something of you.' He put himself at the head of the Enniskillens and led them in the charge.

William's personal gallantry at the battle of the Boyne became a legend; he seemed to be everywhere. A bullet struck his pistol holster; another shot the heel from one of his boots. Whenever his men were driven back he arrived on the scene as though by magic, rallied them and led them forward again.

Deprived of the bulk of their Irish infantry, James's men were in a desperate plight. The Irish cavalry and the French regiments fought superbly. But it could not last long, and gradually at first, and then more quickly, William's army pressed forward until the moment came when their enemy was in full flight.

Little was seen of King James at the battle, and long before it was over, while his Irish cavalry and French infantry were still fighting back against overwhelming odds, he rode back to Dublin as fast as he could. Three days later he was on his way to France, where he lived in exile for the rest of his life.

The defection of the Irish infantry is a mystery. The gallantry of Irish soldiers is proverbial. Many of those who failed at the Boyne fought for Louis of France in his famous Irish Brigade, and became the finest troops in Europe. The Irish regiments in the British Army won glory in battle for two hundred and fifty years.

The casualties at the Boyne were lighter than might be expected for a battle of such importance. Fifteen hundred Irish fell, almost all of them in the cavalry. The losses in the French regiments were about a thousand. The total casualties in the Protestant

Army were less than five hundred, but among them was the great Count Schomberg, killed in the midst of the battle.

In striking contrast to the savage vengeance meted out to Monmouth's men five years before, King William gave strict orders that there should be no bloodshed after the battle. One soldier who killed three Irishmen who asked for quarter, was, by King William's orders, hanged on the spot.

Three days later, William marched into Dublin in triumph. The battle of the Boyne had made the Protestant succession in England safe, and established King William III and Queen Mary II securely on the throne. England had confirmed its will to be a Protestant land. The dreams of Louis XIV of France of a vassal Roman Catholic England were brought to naught. The 1st July has been joyously celebrated ever since by Irish Protestants – the 'Orangemen' – in memory of William of Orange and his great victory at the Battle of the Boyne.

Chapter 14

'The King Over the Water'

The Battle of Culloden

16th April 1746

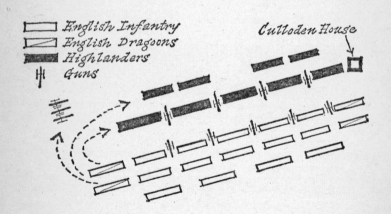

Culloden was the last battle fought on British soil, and it was the last challenge for the British crown. It ended the claim of the House of Stuart and since then the title of the king or queen has never been questioned. To understand Culloden we must go back fifty-six years, to the battle of the Boyne.

When William III defeated the Irish and French army at the Boyne in 1690 King James II went into exile in France. He never surrendered his claim and before he died in 1701 he obtained the promise of Louis XIV of France to recognise his son as king of Scotland and England. This was done and the thirteen-year-old Prince James Edward Francis Stuart, later known as 'The Old Pretender, was proclaimed, in France, King James VIII of Scotland and III of England'. The English Parliament was so angry at this presumption that it immediately voted funds to William for war against France and Spain.

It will be remembered that King William III and Queen Mary II reigned jointly, as both had a right to the throne (see the family tree on page 143). Mary died in 1694 and William in 1702, leaving no children. James Edward, living in exile in France, was too young at fourteen to try to obtain the succession, and his champion, the King of France, had died in 1701. The succession therefore passed easily to Queen Mary's sister, the second daughter of James II, who became Queen Anne. Although young James Edward was out of the picture, Britain was still ruled by a Stuart queen. When James Edward was eighteen he made a bid for the crown of his half-sister. He left France with a small French fleet and troops, but the British fleet was ready, one ship was captured and young James Edward and his supporters had to go back to France.

The trouble over the succession to the crown became serious when Queen Anne died in 1714. Again there was no direct heir to the throne and the exiled James was the obvious successor. He was, however, a Roman Catholic and Protestant Britain would not consider him. It will be remembered that James II was rejected in 1688 because he was a Roman Catholic. So Queen Anne was succeeded by George, Elector, or Prince, of Hanover, who became King George I. His right to the crown is best understood by looking at the family tree on page 143, where it will be seen that he was the great-grandson of James I, through his mother and grandmother.

George I was only a minor German Prince, descended from James I through the maternal side, and he could not speak a word of English. But he was a Protestant and the choice was made because it held the least threat of civil war, a catastrophe from which England had suffered much in the past. That it was a wise choice is shown by the fact that the descendants of George I have reigned in Britain ever since.

The accession of George I was not welcomed by everyone; there was a minority in Britain, known as the Jacobites, who remained loyal to the House of Stuart. They were thick in Scotland and were scattered about England, and included politicians disgruntled with the government. They plotted and dreamed and drank the health of 'The King over the Water', the twenty-six-year-old exile at St Germain in France.

The principal stronghold of the Jacobites was the Highlands of Scotland. There the clansmen lived a wild and often lawless life which belonged to a bygone age. Politically they were behind the times. The more civilised part of Scotland, the Lowlands centred around Edinburgh and Glasgow, had accepted the Act of Union of 1707 which made the two nations one as equal partners.

The Highlanders would not recognise it, and looked to the son of James II to return and claim his own.

Open rebellion broke out when the Earl of Mar, who had helped to frame the Act of Union, set up the standard of James Edward at Braemar on 6th September, 1715, and proclaimed him King James III of Great Britain. Other Highland chiefs followed the lead, proclaiming James at Aberdeen, Dunkeld, Gordon Castle, Brechin, Montrose and Dundee. The Jacobites in Perth seized the town and flew the Stuart standard. The whole of the Highlands was in arms, and within a few weeks the Earl of Mar was commanding eight thousand men and occupied Perth. The fortunate capture of a convoy of arms and gunpowder bound for Sunderland conveniently stocked their magazines.

In London Parliament was swift to act. A reward of £100,000 was offered to anyone capturing the Pretender James Stuart, dead or alive. Emergency acts were passed for the suppression of riots or risings and suspected persons were imprisoned. The Duke of Argyll was appointed Commander-in-Chief in Scotland and with eighteen hundred men took up a strategic position at Stirling, thirty-five miles south of Perth, to control the fords over the River Forth. British regiments were hastily sent to Scotland from England, Ireland and Holland. These were not the scratch troops raised for the emergency as in civil wars in the past, they were regular regiments of the British army, the army which had won resounding victories under the Duke of Marlborough.

Throughout October, 1715, the Earl of Mar was inactive at Perth, except for one unsuccessful dash to try to capture Edinburgh Castle. He was waiting for James to come from France, but when the Pretender did not come to lead his army, Mar marched southwards from Perth on 10th November. He believed that Argyll would not leave his strong and important position at Stirling, so that he could slip past him to Edinburgh.

Directly Argyll learned that Mar had left Perth he marched northwards to meet the Jacobite army. He found ideal ground for his purpose north of Dunblane, which is six miles from Stirling. He took up position with his eight battalions of infantry and three of cavalry with his right flank on Sheriffmuir where the slope of the Ochill hills would favour his cavalry, which he posted on the two flanks of his line. His total strength was only three thousand, for English regiments were on duty elsewhere in Scotland.

The Earl of Mar halted about a mile short of Argyll's line and on the night of 12th November, 1715, both armies slept on their arms, within sound of each other. At dawn they made final preparations and the Duke of Argyll rode along his line, heartening his men, put himself at the head of the cavalry on his right, drew his sword and led them in a charge against the Highlander's left. The Scots cavalry were broken and pursued by the Greys, but the 4th Dragoons, meeting a steady volley from the Highland infantry, were checked and driven back. They charged again, got among the infantry and after some fierce hand-to-hand fighting broke them, chasing them for two miles as far as the River Allan.

Success for the English on the right was matched by success for the Highlanders on their right, where the English were broken and flew back to Stirling. By the time the two successful flank troops returned to the battle they found that a state of stalemate had developed. The Highlanders had withdrawn to a strong hill position and the English were still in front of Dunblane. Neither side attacked and night fell. In the morning the Highlanders had melted away. Sheriffmuir was an indecisive battle, both sides claiming the victory. But the Highland army was scattered and the English troops waited for them to try again. No further attempt was made. James Edward landed at Peterhead, north of Aberdeen, in December and found no army to fight for him. A few weeks later he went on board ship again and returned to France, and George I was secure and unchallenged on the throne of England.

The Old Pretender made no further attempts to regain the crown of England and his cause began to die in England. In the Highlands, however, the Jacobites remained firm in their dreams of a Stuart restoration, recalling the memory of gracious and kindly kings – memory tinged by romance. In Rome the court of the self-styled King James III had a new hope in the person of the Old Pretender's son, Charles Edward. The boy was brought up to believe that England was ruled by a cruel tyrant, and that all the English waited hopefully for the day when they would be set free from the harsh rule of Hanover by their true king.

Charles Edward, 'The Young Pretender', grew up into an engaging and attractive young man, whose head was full of dreams of winning back his father's kingdom. In 1745, when he was twenty-five, his chance came. Britain was at war with France, and that gave him a double advantage. France would welcome civil war in Britain to handicap her war effort, and most of the British Army would be away. The Young Pretender sailed from France with a handful of companions in an eighteen-gun frigate, the *Du Teillay*, accompanied by the sixty-gun *Elizabeth*. After a few days they met the British warship *Lion*, and the *Elizabeth* was so badly mauled that she had to return to France. The *Du Teillay* evaded the British man-of-war and sailed on alone, round Land's End and up the western coast of Britain to the Outer Hebrides, where Charles Edward landed at Eriskay. His ship took him to Loch-na-Nuagh, where he and his companions landed and, in a gesture to show that he had come to stay, sent the ship back to France.

Charles received support from the Highland clans at once. He raised his father's standard at Glenfinnan, at the head of Loch Shiel, on August 19th, and proclaimed him King James VIII of Scotland and III of England. It was a romantic heart-stirring scene, amid the wild and lovely scenery of the western Highlands, as the handsome and princely young man unfurled the Royal Standard. Within a week Charles commanded more than two thousand men, all Highlanders, hard campaigners and splendid fighters. His hopes were high, especially as he imagined that hearts would be equally stirred all over Britain, where Jacobites would, he thought, be preparing to rise against George II of Hanover.

Charles marched boldly to Perth, and from there right into Edinburgh. The city received him well, but the castle, impregnable on its hill, closed its gates and defiantly flew the flag of King George. Occasionally the great guns fired in grim warning. Charles lived in the Palace of Holyrood-house, with his small

Court, but he began to discern dark clouds on the horizon. As he had marched through the Lowlands very few had joined him, and people had seemed to be more in fear of the wild Highlanders than joyous at his coming. For all the cheers in the streets of Edinburgh only three hundred recruits had joined him. There was no news of any Jacobites rising in England. People were behaving in a strange manner for a nation suffering under the heel of a tyrant.

Three armies were in motion against the rising. In Scotland Sir John Cope with two thousand men had marched north from Stirling, had missed the Jacobites and was returning to Edinburgh from Aberdeen by sea. General Wade had a force in the north of England, based at Newcastle, and a third army was in the Midlands. Cope disembarked at Dunbar, thirty miles east of Edinburgh and marched on the city, camping for the night of 20th September near Prestonpans. Charles marched to meet him and the two armies passed the night half-a-mile apart. Charles was on a hill, Cope on a plain between the hill and the sea.

Charles took the initiative in a manner typical of his high-spirited nature. Before sunrise on 21st September, 1745, he led his Highlanders down the hill in a furious and sudden charge on the left wing of the English, taking them quite unawares. In a quarter of an hour Cope's force of two thousand was utterly defeated, and Charles had captured his six guns and his treasure chest. He returned to Edinburgh in triumph.

The victory raised the spirits of the Highlanders, but it had no effect in England; there was still no news whatsoever of Jacobite risings in the south. Unable to wait in Edinburgh for ever Charles decided, against the opinion of some of his officers, to take the bold course and march straight for London. He believed that once he was among them the English would rally to their 'true prince', and that the British soldiers would refuse to fire on him. He had entered Edinburgh easily; he would do the same in London.

The Young Pretender led his army across the border into England on 9th November, 1745. It was a brave and exciting adventure. He marched on foot at the head of the column, now five thousand strong; the handsome and daring 'Bonnie Prince Charlie' marching to challenge the redcoats of King George II to win back his father's kingdom. They cleverly dodged General Wade's army, and took the western route, as Charles II had done ninety-four years before. They besieged and captured Carlisle and marched through Penrith to Preston and south to Manchester. Their reception was good, and three hundred recruits joined at Manchester. Charles was so elated that he asked his officers whether he should enter London mounted or on foot, and what he should wear for the occasion.

They entered Derby on 4th December, and the tune changed. Charles wanted to go on, heartened by the news of a panic in London where people were packing up so that they could get away quickly. His officers wanted to go back to Scotland. Their arguments were too sensible to be disregarded. Three armies in England were marching to unite and bar his passage. There had been no sign of any Jacobite rising in England. There was no sign of an invasion by the French. The officers asked Charles to produce a single letter from someone of importance in the British government with promise of support. If he could do that, they said, they would go on. Charles had no promise of support. There was another difficulty; his army was being reduced steadily as Highlanders, rich with booty, slipped away to go home. This desertion, the officers explained, would increase as they marched southwards.

Sadly Charles had to agree and on 6th December the army marched out of Derby, northwards. This time Charles rode his horse at the rear of the long column. It was a sad end to a brave venture, brave but ill-considered and founded on dreams. They reached Glasgow on 27th December after nearly eight weeks of continuous marching. There was good news to compensate for the retreat; while Charles had been away other clans had come out to fight for him and a force of seven hundred Scottish soldiers, who had been in the service of the King of France had landed, with nineteen field guns.

After a few days' rest in Glasgow Charles marched north and laid siege of Stirling Castle. An English force under General Hawley advanced from Edinburgh to raise the siege and Charles went to meet it. At Falkirk he brought off another surprise attack and won his second victory. He returned to the siege of Stirling, and a week later the Duke of Cumberland arrived in Edinburgh to take over as Commander-in-Chief.

Cumberland was a son of George II, and he was as young, as vigorous and as good a commander as Charles himself. He had experience of active service on the Continent and he knew how to get the best out of his men. His high rank gave him valuable authority over his officers. Cumberland found his troops in poor spirits. They were mostly recruits, and their morale was low after the Highlanders' successes at Prestonpans and Falkirk. The Duke immediately set about training his men for their task. Hard training and strong leadership had the usual effect and the troops began to feel better. The idea that the savage Highlanders were unconquerable began to disappear.

Cumberland trained the infantry to fight in three ranks, the first kneeling, the second stooping and the third standing up. Thus three-fold fire-power could be brought to bear on the enemy. He also made them engage the enemy to their right-front, to get under the round shields, or targets, of the Highlanders. Many commanders would have waited for the spring before venturing into the Highlands, but Cumberland was determined to march to the attack without delay, hard though the campaign would be.

While Cumberland organised his troops in Edinburgh, Charles fretted to march to attack him, confident that he would be successful. But his officers had other ideas. The Highlanders were deserting all the while and the army was shrinking, especially since the victory at Falkirk which had yielded much booty from the vanquished. There were other reasons; quarrels among the Highland chiefs and resentment at Charles's high-handed manner.

Charles had to give way to his officers. The siege of Stirling was raised and they marched north to Inverness, a good base and a port where French reinforcements could be landed. Fort Augustus, thirty-four miles down Loch Ness, was captured, which made them secure from attack from the south. Charles settled down with his court in Inverness to prepare for the spring when he could raise the clans again and add to them substantial reinforcements from France. There were gay dinners, with candlelight gleaming on polished tables and fine silver. There was music and dancing and gaiety; the grace and charm which belonged to the romantic Stuarts.

The Duke of Cumberland had marched north, too, and spent the month of March in Aberdeen, eighty miles across mountainous country from Inverness. Here he continued the training of his army and tried in vain to find out what his enemy was doing and where they were. But no-one would tell him, or help the redcoat army in any way. On 8th April Cumberland was ready, and he marched north-west from Aberdeen across the harsh country to Nairn, on the Moray Firth, some sixteen miles east of Inverness. He was at the head of ten thousand well-trained and well-equipped troops, and ten guns.

When Charles heard that Cumberland had marched to Nairn, he led his five thousand men eastwards from Inverness, and made his headquarters at Culloden House. His men, dispirited and half-starved, camped on Culloden Moor. The Duke stayed in Nairn, to rest his troops after their hard march, and to celebrate his twenty-fifth birthday. Charles resolved to try a surprise attack for the third time, and formed his men up on the night of the 14th to march the twelve miles to Nairn, there to fall on the English while they were encamped. This time the ruse failed, his men were too weak with hunger to march the twelve miles; they faltered and turned back to Culloden.

The Duke of Cumberland stirred early and his army was under arms and ready to march off at five o'clock in the morning of 16th April, 1746. He halted a short way from Culloden House and put his army into battle formation. Six battalions of infantry and two regiments of dragoons were in the first two lines, with a

Redcoats and Highlanders at the Battle of Culloden, 1746

reserve as the third line. The dragoons were on the flanks and the guns in pairs between the battalions of the front line.

The Duke inspected his battle order, saw that all was right, and addressed the men. 'I don't suppose there are any men here who are disinclined to fight,' he said, 'but if there be any, I beg them in God's name to go, for I would rather face the Highlanders with a thousand resolute men than with ten thousand half-hearted!' The men cheered, which boded ill for the Highlanders.

Charles formed his five thousand, already weary from their ineffectual night march, into two lines, their right covered by small buildings and gardens, their left by Culloden House itself. The Macdonald clan were on the left, in a bad mood because they had expected to have the place of honour on the right. Charles had posted his nineteen guns, against the Duke's ten, in his front line too. Charles began the battle of Culloden with artillery fire, to which Cumberland at once replied. The Duke also sent his dragoons round the Highlanders' right flank to clear them from the scattered cover they had occupied. The Highlanders got the worst of the artillery duel; they fired their guns with poor aim whilst the English gunners, well practised by Cumberland, were accurate. They fired grape-shot, small cannon balls linked together, which caused havoc in the Highland line; so much so that, enraged by the murderous grape-shot, they charged the English line.

Steady volleys, fired on the word of command, and well aimed, slew many Highlanders, but the line surged forward and closed. Soon it was bayonet against claymore. Some Highlanders swept round the left of the British line and fell on the flanking regiments, with such savage fury that they began to fall back. But the regiments steadied, fought back and drove their assailants off with their bayonets.

Meanwhile the English dragoons had fought through on the Highland flank, and four guns were taken up. They opened fire with grape-shot in the Highlanders' second line. The Macdonalds watched the battle, but refused to advance, sulking over their imagined insult. When they did move it was to retreat, for the first line was being driven back by musket fire, and the second line broke under the artillery fire. In a short time the Highlanders were in full retreat, pursued ruthlessly by the dragoons who cut them down as they ran. The victory was complete. More than a thousand Highlanders were killed, five hundred were taken prisoner. In the English army only fifty were killed and about two hundred wounded.

The Highlanders were formed into regiments of the British Army a few years later, where their magnificent fighting spirit was tempered by discipline, to make them among the finest soldiers in the world.

The Duke of Cumberland had done more than defeat the rebel army beyond all chance of recovery. He had overcome the fear in the hearts of the Lowlanders and the English for the fierce and semi-barbarous Highlanders. He had ended for good the disturbing element of the Jacobites in Britain. The young prince had done this by sheer personal qualities. He had trained his men with intelligence and skill, he had led them boldly and he had proved his generalship. After the battle the fugitives were hunted in the mountains, and when people hid Highlanders or refused to help the English, houses were burned. Crops were destroyed and the rebellion was mercilessly stamped out. The Duke's thoroughness and harshness won him the unpleasant nickname of Butcher. It is only fair to the memory of a brave and brilliant young man to remember also the success of his operations and his victory of Culloden, in the last battle fought on British soil.

Charles escaped from the battlefield and spent five months a fugitive in the Highlands. He had many adventures, and was at one time disguised as a woman. The loyalty and devotion of many Highlanders helped him to escape, often narrowly. There are countless stories of the adventures of Bonnie Prince Charlie escaping from Cumberland's redcoats, the most famous of them all concerning the heroine Flora Macdonald. She got him safely to the Isle of Skye. At last a French frigate picked him up, and as *L'Heureux* sailed away on 20th September, 1746, the adventures of the last of the Stuarts were over, and he passed from the pages of history.

Principal Battles Fought in Britain

(Battles told in this book are marked *)

Battle	Remarks
B.C.	
55 Invasion	Reconnaissance by Julius Caesar
54 Invasion	Julius Caesar lands
A.D.	
43 Invasion	Claudius lands
51 Caer Caradoc	Romans defeat Caractacus
61 (Not certain)	Suetonius defeats Queen Boudicca
500 Badon	King Arthur defeats Saxons
871 Ashdown	King Alfred defeats Danes
878 Ethandun	King Alfred finally defeats the Danes
*1066 Stamford Bridge	Harold defeats Norwegians
*1066 Hastings	William conquers England
1138 Battle of the Standard	David I of Scotland defeated at Northallerton
*1264 Lewes	Simon de Montfort defeats Henry III
*1265 Evesham	Prince Edward defeats Simon de Montfort

Battle	*Remarks*
1282 Builth	Edward I completes the conquest of Wales
1296 Dunbar	English defeat Baliol I of Scotland
1298 Falkirk	Edward I defeats William Wallace of Scotland
1307 Loudon Hill	Robert the Bruce of Scotland defeats English army
*1314 Bannockburn	Robert the Bruce defeats Edward II of England
1346 Neville's Cross	English defeat David II of Scotland
1388 Chevy Chase	Scottish victory of Henry Percy, 'Harry Hotspur'
1403 Shrewsbury	Henry IV defeats Harry Hotspur
*1455 St Albans	(Beginning of Wars of the Roses) Victory for York
1459 Blore Heath	Victory for York
1460 Northampton	Victory for York
1460 Wakefield	Victory for Lancaster
1461 Mortimer's Cross	Victory for York
*1461 St Albans	Victory for Lancaster
*1461 Towton	Victory for York
1464 Hedgely Moor	Victory for York
1464 Hexham	Victory for York
1469 Banbury	Victory for Lancaster
1470 Stamford	Victory for York
1471 Barnet	Victory for York
1471 Tewkesbury	Victory for York
*1485 Bosworth	Victory for Lancaster (End of Wars of the Roses)
*1487 Stoke Field	Henry VII defeats the impostor Lambert Simnel

Battle		Remark
1513	Flodden	English army defeats James IV of Scotland
*1642	Edgehill	(Beginning of Civil War) Royalist victory
1643	Chalgrove Field	Royalist victory
1643	Atherton Moor	Royalist victory
1643	Lansdown	Royalist victory
1643	Roundway Down	Royalist victory
1643	Newbury	Parliament victory
1644	Nantwich	Parliament victory
1644	Marston Moor	Parliament victory
1644	Newbury	Indecisive
*1645	Naseby	Parliament victory (End of Civil War)
1650	Dunbar	Parliament defeats the Scots
*1651	Worcester	Parliament defeats Charles II
*1685	Sedgemoor	James II defeats Monmouth
1689	Killiecrankie	England and Scotland, a draw
1689	Londonderry	Unsuccessful siege by James II
*1690	The Boyne	William III defeats James II
1715	Sheriffmuir	English defeat the 'Old Pretender'
1745	Prestonpans	'Young Pretender' defeats an English army
1746	Falkirk	'Young Pretender' defeats an English army
*1746	Culloden	English army finally defeats the 'Young Pretender' (Last battle on British soil)
1940	Battle of Britain	Royal Air Force defeats the German Air Force

Index

More Beaver Books

We hope you have enjoyed this Beaver Book. Here are some of the other titles:

A Knight and his Castle What it was like to live in a castle, by R. Ewart Oakeshott

The Tower and the Traitors The amazing stories of just some of the men and women who have lived and died in the Tower; told by Barbara Leonie Picard

White Fang Jack London's great classic story about the life of a wild wolf dog at the time of the Gold Rush in the Yukon

When Darkness Comes A primitive tribe struggles for survival when torn apart by internal rivalries, but the appearance of a strange enemy makes unity essential. Robert Swindells has written a powerful first novel for older children

The 'Tripods' Trilogy John Christopher's magnificent trilogy about the Masters, terrifying invaders from outer space who control the world by dominating men's minds. The three books in order are *The White Mountains*, *The City of Gold and Lead* and *The Pool of Fire*

Picture Puzzles Ninety-six pages packed with a variety of brain-teasers, including mazes, 'spot-the-difference' and 'I spy' games, written and illustrated by Walter Shepherd

New Beavers are published every month and if you would like the *Beaver Bulletin* – which gives all the details – please send a large stamped addressed envelope to:

Beaver Bulletin
The Hamlyn Group
Astronaut House
Feltham
Middlesex TW14 9AR

314049